To Colleen! — !
Have Fun Cooking!

Teri SANDISON

Also by Hugh Carpenter and Teri Sandison

Wok Fast
Fast Appetizers
Hot Chicken
Hot Pasta
Hot Barbecue
Hot Vegetables
Hot Wok
The Great Ribs Book

Fast Entrées

Hugh Carpenter

and Teri Sandison

CHARTWELL
BOOKS

This edition published in 2015 by
CHARTWELL BOOKS
an imprint of Book Sales
a division of Quarto Publishing Group USA Inc.
142 West 36th Street, 4th Floor
New York, New York 10018
USA

Printed with permission of and by arrangement with Ten Speed Press.

Cover and text design by Beverly Wilson
Food styling by Julie Smith
Typography by Laurie Harty

Library of Congress Cataloging-in-Publication Data

Carpenter, Hugh.
Fast entrées / Hugh Carpenter and Teri Sandison.
        p. cm.
Includes index.
ISBN-13: 978-0-7858-3213-3

1. Entrées (Cookery) I. Sandison, Teri. II. Title.
TX740 .C312   2002
641.8'2—dc21   2002000548

Printed in China

1 2 3 4 5 6 7 8 9 10

To Robert and Sally Hunt,

who gather family and friends around the table

every night. Thank you

for enriching our lives

in so many ways.

Contents

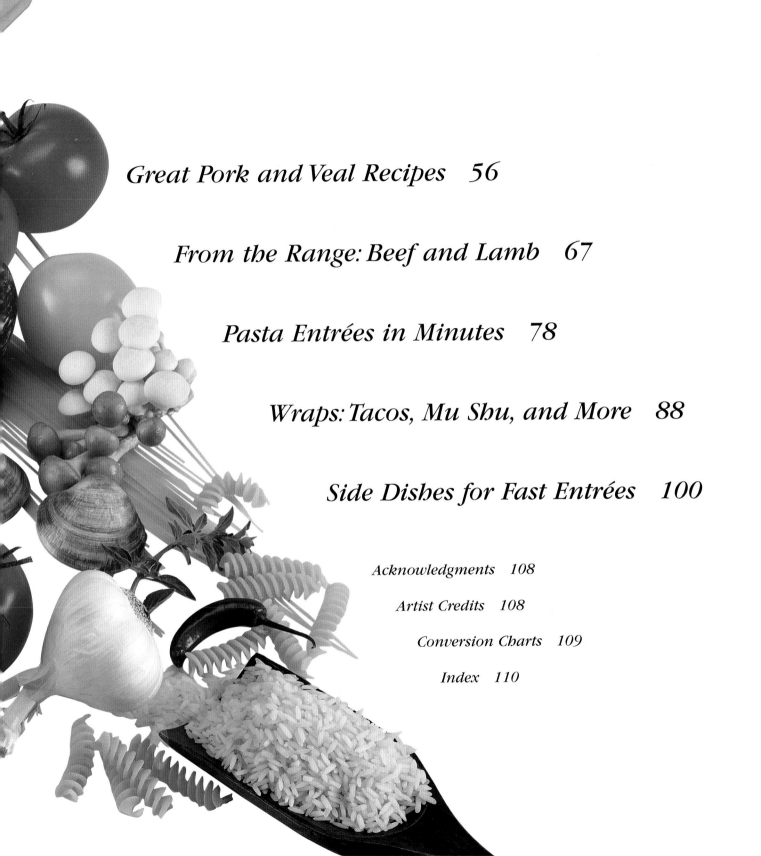

Fast Entrées for Every Occasion

Home-cooked dinners are one of life's great pleasures. But these days, many of us are so caught up in the goings-on of everyday life that we find our cooking time reduced to practically nothing. It often seems easier to eat take-out food, frozen dinners, and the heavily processed products lining market shelves.

We have long felt that great home-cooked dinners are not dependent on endless chopping, rare ingredients, fancy pots and pans, and gourmet cooking skills. Night after night, we build our meal around a fast-to-prepare entrée made with fresh ingredients. A typical week might include pan-fried sole served with lemon wedges and tartar sauce; chicken marinated and roasted with barbecue sauce; and pasta with steamed mussels and a store-bought pesto sauce.

Quality ingredients are the foundation for great-tasting, simply prepared entrées. Start with the best, and lengthy preparations become superfluous. Purchase the freshest possible meat, seafood, and vegetables. Cook the food within two days to capture its peak flavor. Accent it with premium spices, condiments, oils, and vinegars. If you season broiled fresh fish with freshly ground black pepper, a sprinkling of salt, and a drizzle of balsamic vinegar, the result will be an intensely satisfying fast entrée.

Match a fast entrée with a crusty baguette, Chinese-style steamed rice, or pasta tossed with a premium pasta sauce and a sprinkling of imported Parmesan cheese. In our home, if Hugh makes the entrée, then Teri prepares a dinner salad or a vegetable side dish either starting from scratch or utilizing what's ready-cut from the market.

For work-night dinners, we never serve meat or seafood entrées with both *a vegetable course and a salad. This is unnecessary nutritionally and gastronomically. By preparing either a salad or a vegetable side dish, you'll have more time to enjoy a leisurely dinner.*

Make use of what's available at the market to simplify your side dishes. You can find a vast number of packaged grains and pastas; breads, rolls, and tortillas; refrigerated salad mixes; and excellent designer salad dressings. Often we'll slightly embellish a market product to give it a homemade taste. We'll stir toasted nuts into a rice pilaf, squeeze lemon juice into couscous, or intensify a salad dressing with a squeeze of lime juice, dashes of chile sauce, and some chopped herbs. But we think you'll find that the side dish recipes provided in this book are as easy to make as most store-bought products.

A note on the recipes: each one provides advance preparation instructions. On most nights, we'll be heating up the oven, warming a sauté pan, or lighting a barbecue fire while completing these prep steps. But if you prefer to complete the preparation ahead of time, it can be done up to 8 hours in advance of cooking. All the recipes also provide menu suggestions, and often refer to our easy side dishes. Take these as starting points for surrounding your entrées with simple dishes that play a supporting role.

We invite you to join us on the endlessly satisfying adventure of simple home cooking. Read through the chapter on cooking techniques, review the suggested side dishes, and choose a couple of fast entrées to make over the next few nights. Gather your family and friends. Let these fast, flavor-intense recipes be the catalyst for lively dinners night after night. It's one of the easiest and most wonderful ways to enrich the lives of those we love.

Hugh Carpenter and Teri Sandison

The Essential Pantry

Good cooking begins with great ingredients. This means not only purchasing the freshest vegetables, seafood, meat, and herbs, but also choosing the best types of oils, vinegars, Asian condiments, and other seasonings. Buy the highest quality whenever possible. The best brands of Asian condiments are rarely found in American markets, but are readily found in Chinese, Vietnamese, and Thai markets. If you're unsure about where to look, ask the owner of your favorite Asian restaurant for recommendations on where to find the best Asian markets.

Chile Flakes, Crushed Red: Sold in the spice section of all markets, and appearing on the table at pizza restaurants, these chile flakes are usually labeled "crushed red pepper."

Chiles, Fresh: The most commonly sold fresh chiles are serrano and jalapeño. Use them to add heat to any recipe, or as a substitute for chile sauce. To use, trim off the stem, and then mince the chile, without removing the seeds, in an electric mini-chopper. If you prefer less heat, you can discard the seeds before chopping.

Anchovy Paste: A combination of puréed anchovies, vinegar, garlic, and spices, anchovy paste is sold in small tubes. It adds a rich taste without the strong anchovy flavor that so many people find objectionable.

Bread Crumbs, Dry: Sold in every supermarket, we prefer the unseasoned type. Japanese bread crumbs, called panko, are coarser, resulting in a crunchy crust.

Butter: Always use unsalted butter, never margarine or other fake butters. Substitutes: Flavorless cooking oils, such as peanut, safflower, corn, or olive oil.

Capers: The flower bud of a bush native to the Mediterranean and parts of Asia, capers are sold pickled in a vinegar brine. Rinse before using.

Cheeses: There are many small manufacturers of excellent American goat cheese (such as Laura Chenel) and blue cheese (Maytag blue), but American-produced Parmesan cheese has a scalded-milk taste. For Parmesan, always buy Italian Parmigiano-Reggiano cheese.

Chicken Broth: While we prefer using the frozen chicken broth available at some supermarket delis, all the recipes in this book will taste fine using a store-bought low-sodium chicken broth.

Chile Sauce, Asian: This is a general term covering many Asian chile sauces, variously labeled as "chile paste," "chile sauce," and "chile paste with garlic." Refrigerate after opening. Best brand: Rooster Delicious Hot Chile Garlic Sauce. Substitute: Your favorite hot sauce.

Chili Powder: A blend of chiles and many different spices processed into a powder and sold in the spice section of every supermarket. Used for making American-style chili.

Chipotle Chiles in Adobo Sauce: These smoked jalapeños simmered in a spicy sauce are sold in 4-ounce tins at every Mexican market and in many American supermarkets. To use, finely mince the chiles, including the seeds, and use along with the sauce. A word of warning: these are extremely spicy! To store, transfer to a glass or Tupperware container and refrigerate. Lasts indefinitely.

Fish Sauce, Thai or Vietnamese: Pungent, salty fish sauce, made by fermenting anchovies or other fish in brine, is as ubiquitous in Thai and Vietnamese cooking as soy sauce is in Chinese cooking. Purchase fish sauce produced in Thailand or Vietnam, since they have the lowest salt content. Once opened, fish sauce lasts indefinitely at room temperature. Best brands: Three Crab, Phu Quoc Flying Lion, or Tiparos. Thin soy sauce can be substituted for fish sauce, although the flavor is quite different.

Ginger, Fresh: These knobby brown roots are sold by all supermarkets in the produce section. Finely minced, ginger is a great addition to many non-Asian dishes such as guacamole, salsa, and fish chowder. Buy firm ginger with smooth skin. Peeling ginger is unnecessary unless the skin is wrinkled. Store uncut ginger in the refrigerator at room temperature. There is no substitute for fresh ginger.

Hoisin Sauce: This is one of the Asian condiments most loved by Americans. A thick and sweet, spicy, dark sauce, it is made with soy beans, chiles, garlic, ginger, and sugar. Once opened, it keeps indefinitely at room temperature. Best brand: Koon Chun Hoisin Sauce. There is no substitute for hoisin sauce.

Coconut Milk: Canned coconut milk is available in Asian markets and many supermarkets. It is used more for the consistency it gives sauces than for its subtle flavor. Look for brands with just coconut and water listed as ingredients. Stir or shake the coconut milk well before using. Once opened, coconut milk is highly perishable and should be refrigerated no longer than one week. It can also be frozen. Best brand: Chaokoh from Thailand. Never substitute low-fat coconut milk, which has an off taste.

Five-Spice Powder: A powdered blend of anise, fennel, cinnamon, Szechuan pepper, and cloves, it is available at most supermarkets and all Asian markets.

Garlic: Always use fresh garlic and mince it yourself (see page 14), rather than purchasing prepared minced garlic, garlic paste, or garlic powder.

Herbs, Fresh: Available throughout the year at most supermarkets, fresh herbs have a far more intense bouquet than their dried counterparts. To prepare most fresh herbs, separate the leaves from the stems, discard the stems, and then chop or mince the leaves. The exception to this procedure is cilantro, for which both the stems and the leaves should be used, hence you'll see that we call for minced cilantro sprigs rather than leaves. In an emergency, dried herbs can be substituted for fresh herbs, using about half the amount of fresh herbs specified.

Hot Sauce, Your Favorite: Use an Asian chile sauce (see above), or any spicy chile sauce from around the world. Don't select a simple tomato-based sauce—the spice is good!

Mustard, Honey and Dijon: While we don't have specific brands to recommend, we do suggest that you avoid the inferior tasting American-made bright yellow mustard. The more expensive brands are higher in quality, and therefore taste better.

Oil: In this book, we call for a variety of different oils. For sautéing and general cooking, use mild-flavored vegetable oils, such as peanut, safflower, and corn oils. Extra virgin olive oil smokes at a low temperature, so is often used for flavor rather than cooking. Plain olive oil has a higher smoking point, so is used in recipes where extra virgin won't perform well. Plain olive oil and flavorless cooking oils can be used interchangeably.

Oyster Sauce: This Asian cooking sauce, also called "oyster-flavored sauce," gives a rich taste to a dish without a hint of its seafood origins. We use it in many European dishes in place of salt. It will keep indefinitely in the refrigerator. Best brands: Sa Cheng Oyster Flavored Sauce; Hop Sing Lung Oyster Sauce; and Lee Kum Kee Oyster Flavored Sauce, Old Brand. There is no substitute, but oyster sauce is widely available in supermarkets and Asian markets.

Pita Bread: A Middle Eastern pocket bread made of white or whole wheat flour, pita bread is available at most American supermarkets.

Plum Sauce: This chutney-like sauce is made with plums, apricots, garlic, red chiles, sugar, vinegar, salt, and water. It makes a great foundation for barbecue sauces. Plum sauce is available at most supermarkets and Asian food stores. Once opened, it will keep indefinitely in the refrigerator. Best brand: Koon Chun Plum Sauce. Substitute: your favorite chutney.

Sesame Oil, Dark: This is a nutty, dark golden-brown oil made from toasted and crushed white sesame seeds. Do not mistake dark sesame oil for the clear-colored sesame oil made from untoasted seeds, which has no flavor; or for "black sesame oil," which has an overwhelmingly strong taste. Dark sesame oil is used in small amounts just to add flavor to Asian dishes, but never as a cooking oil since it smokes at a low temperature. Dark sesame oil will last for at least a year at room temperature, and indefinitely in the refrigerator. Best brand: Kadoya Sesame Oil.

Olives and Tapenade: Olives purchased with the pit still intact are less salty and have a more intense olive taste than pitted imported olives. For the small amount of olives needed in most recipes, it doesn't take long to dislodge the pit yourself, especially if you have an olive pitter. If you don't have an olive pitter, gently crush the olives with the side of a knife, and then extract the pit. Never use American canned olives, which have been chemically processed. Tapenade is a thick paste made from olives, garlic, and seasonings.

Peppercorns, Green: These are soft, unripe peppercorn berries that are sold both dried and submerged in brine. If in brine, rinse before using. The peppercorns should be minced in an electric mini-chopper rather than a mortar and pestle, which leaves larger pieces.

Red Peppers, Roasted: Red bell peppers take on a wonderful sweet, smoky flavor when roasted, peeled, and seeded. They are available bottled, sold alongside the pickles and relishes at every supermarket. To roast your own, see page 39.

Sesame Seeds, White: These small white seeds can add a subtle, nutty flavor to a variety of dishes. Look for them in the spice section of every American supermarket. Avoid pretoasted sesame or brown seeds, which are inferior in taste.

Soy Sauce, Dark: Also labeled "heavy" or "black," this soy sauce has slightly more body than regular soy sauce due to the addition of molasses. Dark soy sauce will add more flavor and color to food than thin soy sauce. Best brand: Mushroom Soy Sauce.

Sherry, Dry: Asian cooks would use rice wine, not sherry, but it is only available at Asian markets. Inexpensive dry sherry, Japanese sake, or dry vermouth make good substitutes. A good brand of Chinese rice wine (not to be confused with rice wine vinegar) is Pagoda Shao Xing Rice Wine.

Soy Sauce, Thin: "Thin" or "light" soy sauce is a mildly salty liquid made from soybeans, roasted wheat, yeast, and salt. If you are concerned about sodium, decrease the quantity of soy sauce in a recipe or use a naturally made low-sodium brand. Best brands: Pearl River Bridge Golden Label Superior Soya Sauce, Koon Chun Thin Soy Sauce, or Kikkoman Regular Soy Sauce.

Tomato Sauce: The best-tasting brands of bottled tomato sauces are Classico, Newman's Own, Muir Glen, and Coppola.

Tortillas, Flour and Corn: Always buy fresh tortillas when available. Frozen tortillas have an inferior taste. You'll find the best tortillas at Latin markets.

Vinegars: Japanese rice vinegar has 4 to 5 percent acidity, as compared to American and European vinegar with 6 to 7 percent acidity, and the very mild Chinese vinegar with 2.5 percent acidity. If a recipe calls for rice vinegar but all you have is a European vinegar, use a little less than the recipe specifies. Rice vinegar is available at most American supermarkets.

With these essential pantry ingredients on hand, it takes only seconds to add a splash or dash of flavor to a dish, elevating it from mundane to inspired.

Time-Saving Equipment and Techniques

Grating and Shredding Cheese

Grate hard cheeses, such as Parmesan, using a hand grater or grating wheel, or cut into small pieces and, with the motor running, drop down the feed tube of a food processor. Shred softer cheeses, such as mozzarella, using a hand grater or the shredding blade of a food processor.

Grating Citrus Zest

Use the citrus grater or microplane called the "Great Zester," as shown in photograph.

Juicing Citrus

For extracting small amounts of juice quickly, both reamers and squeeze juicers work well.

Peeling and Mincing Garlic

Remove the skin by using a rubber garlic tube. Mince by forcing through a garlic press or processing in an electric mini-chopper. Best garlic press: Zyliss.

Mincing Ginger

Peel ginger only if the skin is wrinkled. Wash and dry. Cut the ginger crosswise in *paper-thin* slices. Stand the slices on edge in a Zyliss Garlic Press and then press the plunger down, or mince in an electric mini-chopper. Best mini-choppers: Krups and Cuisinart.

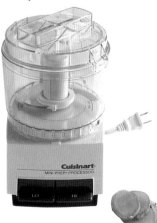

Mincing Green Onions

Double the onions back and forth, then mince. Or tear into small pieces and, with the motor running, drop down the feed tube of a food processor.

Mincing Herbs

Gather the herbs into a bunch under your fingers, cut thinly, then mince. Do not mince herbs in a mini-chopper or food processor because the blade will tear and blacken the leaves.

Grating Nutmeg

Freshly ground nutmeg has the best flavor. To grate nutmeg, use a grater made specifically for the purpose. The fine holes of a cheese grater can also be used.

Pitting Olives

Two superior olive pitters we've used are the Westmark and Pedrini models.

Grinding Spices

Always use an electric coffee grinder that is used only for this purpose.

Knives

For an all-purpose knife, we prefer the Global Vegetable Chopper (Model #GF-36). It's perfect for mincing, chopping, and slicing all meat, seafood, and vegetables. This knife should never be used for cutting through bones, which will ruin the blade. Other good all-purpose knives are European chef's knives and the lightweight Chinese cleaver made by Martin Yan. You should also have several paring knives on hand, as these are extremely useful. Less frequently used but indispensable are a boning knife and a serrated knife.

Diamond Steel Knife Sharpener

A diamond steel is the best sharpening tool for maintaining knives or putting a new edge on a dull one. Any cookware shop can show you how to use the steel properly. Our favorite is the DMT Sharpening Steel.

Meat Pounder

Meat pounders are used to flatten boneless chicken breasts and veal scaloppine. The pounder should be smooth on the side that comes into contact with the meat.

Instant-Read Meat Thermometer

Of the dozens of meat thermometers, battery-operated ones with long probes are the most accurate and practical. The best thermometers are made by Component Design (CDN) and Poleer.

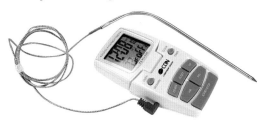

Poultry Shears

Poultry shears make trimming raw poultry or portioning cooked poultry a snap! The best brand is Joyce Chen.

Cooking Techniques: The Basics

BARBECUING

*T*hroughout this book, we use the common meaning of "barbecue"—to cook food directly or indirectly over a bed of coals or flames. Barbecuing is the easiest way to create complex tasting dishes with a minimum of preparation time and only occasional supervision during cooking. Barbecuing traps juices, browns and crisps exteriors, concentrates and caramelizes marinades, and infuses food with unique smoky essences.

To add an intense additional flavor to barbecued food, soak 1 cup of wood chips in cold water for 30 minutes. Preheat your grill, then drain and place the chips on a layer of aluminum foil positioned at one corner of the grill rack. When the wood begins to smoke, place the food on the rack and cover with the top.

"Barbecue" and "incinerate" are not synonymous! Always barbecue over medium heat. Place your open hand, palm side down, four inches above the heat, and count "1001, 1002, 1003." The heat is medium if you are forced to remove your hand at "1003." The food should make a slight sizzling noise throughout the cooking. Turn the meat or seafood several times during cooking, brushing on more of the marinade you are using. For food safety, set aside a small amount of marinade for basting *before* adding the meat or seafood to the marinade. Whenever you're not turning the food over, cover the barbecue so the aromatic smoke is trapped inside.

It's always better to undercook food than overcook it; you can always put food back on the barbecue for further cooking, but there's no remedy for overcooking. In short, baby the food: prod it, nudge it, brush it, and err on the side of undercooking.

Barbecue equipment: oven mitt, offset spatula, instant-read meat thermometer, water spritzer, brush, and tongs.

BROILING

*B*roiling is a perfect cooking technique for fast entrées. However, because of the high heat used, it's crucial to continually monitor what's going on in the oven. Please, no cocktails in the other room while broiling!

In gas and newer electric ovens, once turned on, the broiler will stay on continuously when the oven door is closed. Broilers in older electric ovens turn off once the oven temperature rises above 500°F. Sometimes people open the door to force the broiler to stay on, but this allows too much heat to escape. An easy solution is to leave the oven door slightly ajar by closing it on a wooden spoon. The small opening will allow just enough heat to escape to keep the broiler on while keeping the oven chamber hot.

To Broil Fish: The following technique combines broiling with high-temperature roasting. Using this method, fish never scorches, nor does it need to be turned over or lowered to another oven rack. Limit the thickness of the fish to 1½ inches or less.

Position an oven rack 4 inches below the heating element. Preheat the oven to 500°F on the Bake setting. (This preheating assures that when the fish goes under the broiler, the underside of the food will begin cooking at once.) Line a shallow baking dish with aluminum foil and place the fish in the pan.

Once the oven reaches 500°F, turn the setting to Broil. If you have the optional oven settings of Convection Broil or High Broil, use either of these. When the broiler coil glows or the gas flames light, place the fish in the oven. For gas and new electric ovens, close the door. For older electric ovens, crack the door open.

When the fish is golden on top, check for doneness. If it's not fully cooked, turn the oven setting back to Bake at 500°F. Shut the oven door if it's been cracked open during broiling. Continue cooking the fish at 500°F until it flakes with slight pressure from a fork. If the fish is an inch or more thick, monitor the cooking by using an instant-read meat thermometer such as one of the brands recommended on page 15. The fish is done when it registers 130°F on the thermometer.

To Broil Meat: For meat such as steaks, chops, and hamburgers, it's unnecessary to preheat the oven prior to broiling. Just turn the broiler on, and place the meat 4 inches from the heating element. Once the meat becomes golden, turn it over and broil on the other side until browned. If the meat has not reached the desired internal temperature, change the oven setting to Bake at 275 to 300°F, and finish the cooking at this temperature.

Broiling meat or fish: Place on a shallow baking dish lined with foil.

ROASTING

*A*lthough roasting is typically considered a slow method of cooking, smaller cuts of poultry and meat roast quite quickly, with flavorful results. Roasting is a great technique for pieces of chicken, halved game hens, whole pork tenderloin, and rack of lamb. Be sure to use a heavy roasting pan or baking dish so that it doesn't buckle during cooking. Unless the meat is cooked with fruit or vegetables nestled around it (as with the pork tenderloin dish on page 64), it should always be roasted on a wire rack placed in the pan. Racks allow for better air circulation around the meat, which creates even cooking and browning.

Roasting: Line a shallow baking dish with aluminum foil. Place a wire rack in the pan. Coat the rack with nonstick spray and place the meat on the rack.

SAUTÉING

*F*or creative cooks, sautéing is an action-packed technique where the sizzling oil, changes in food color, and dramatic aromas determine the timing. The hot sauté pan seals the juices inside the food and rapidly transfers heat from the food's surface to its interior. Because sautéing should be done just prior to serving, the technique is best used for small gatherings of family and friends. Use a 12- or 14-inch heavy sauté pan, such as those manufactured by Viking, SilverStone, All-Clad, and Calphalon.

1. Place a sauté pan over high heat. When the pan is hot, add just enough cooking oil to create a film across the surface of the pan. When the oil begins to smoke, add the food, giving the pan a slight jiggle to distribute the oil underneath.

2. Adjust the heat so the oil is always sizzling but does not smoke. When the food is lightly brown on one side, turn over. If adding a sauce, remove the food from the pan and discard any excess oil.

3. Add the sauce to the pan and bring to a boil. Return the food to the pan and decrease the heat to achieve a simmer. For food over ½ inch thick, cover the pan and simmer until the ingredients are cooked through. If the sauce flavor needs to be concentrated or if the sauce needs to be thickened, transfer the food to warmed dinner plates. Boil the sauce vigorously over high heat, then spoon over the food.

STIR-FRYING

*S*tir-frying involves searing a small amount of food in a very hot pan so that all the flavors are locked inside while the exterior is glazed with a wonderful sauce. Use a flat bottomed 14- or 16-inch-diameter heavy wok with one long wooden handle and a second short handle, or a 14-inch cast-iron frying pan. Keep the heat on high—never decreasing it throughout the cooking process. Never stir-fry more than 1 pound of meat or seafood or 4 cups of vegetables at a time or the pan will be too crowded and the food will become soggy. To stir-fry a larger amount, use two separate woks.

1. Heat the wok over the highest possible heat until very hot. Add peanut, safflower, or corn oil as specified in the recipe to the center of the wok, and roll the oil quickly around the bottom one-third of the wok. If the oil isn't added quickly, and then quickly rolled around the wok, the oil will begin to smoke heavily and may burst into flames. If the oil flames, cover the wok, and remove it from the heat.

2. When the oil just begins to smoke, gently slide the meat or seafood into the bottom of the wok. Never drop the food into the wok from a height, or the oil will splatter badly.

3. Using a wooden spatula, stir, lift, and turn over the food. Spread the ingredients evenly across the surface in order to sear the food, wait 2 to 5 seconds, and then stir and toss the food again. Follow the recipe's directions for cooking times and visual cues for doneness.

4. If the stir-fry includes meat or seafood plus vegetables, the meat or seafood is stir-fried first and then removed and set aside while the vegetables are stir-fried. When removing food from the wok, shake the wok vigorously to loosen the food, then slide the food out by tipping the wok toward you.

5. When all of the meat, seafood, or vegetables in a recipe have been stir-fried in batches, return all of the ingredients to the wok. Immediately add the wok sauce specified in the recipe, pouring it into the bottom one-third of the wok. Continue stir-frying until the sauce glazes all the ingredients and thickens slightly.

6. Have at the ready a solution of 2 teaspoons cornstarch dissolved in 2 teaspoons cold water. If the sauce appears watery, hold the stir-fry spatula level. Pour about 2 teaspoons of the cornstarch mixture onto the spatula, and then stir this into the wok ingredients. If the sauce does not thicken slightly, then stir in a little more cornstarch solution. When the sauce has thickened, tip the wok toward you, and slide the food onto a heated platter or dinner plates. Serve at once.

Fast Fish

S almon should always be grilled skin side down with the barbecue tightly covered. The skin protects the underside of the salmon without burning away, while the closed lid traps the heat and cooks the top side. If the salmon has been skinned, it should be cooked on aluminum foil: Cut a double layer of aluminum foil to the exact size of the piece of fish. Rub the foil with a little cooking oil to prevent sticking.

Removing pin bones from salmon: *Brush your fingers down the center of the fish until you feel the ridge of pin bones. Using needle-nose pliers or tweezers, pull out each bone with the grain, trying not to tear the flesh.*

Barbecued Salmon, Tuscan-Style

SERVES 4

Tuscan Marinade
6 cloves garlic, finely minced
3 tablespoons extra virgin olive oil
⅓ cup freshly squeezed lemon juice
3 tablespoons honey
⅓ cup pitted imported black or green olives, minced
2 teaspoons chopped fresh rosemary, or 2 tablespoons chopped fresh basil
2 teaspoons anchovy paste, or ½ teaspoon salt
1 teaspoon crushed red pepper flakes

2 pounds fresh salmon fillet, skin on and pin bones removed
2 teaspoons grated orange zest
2 teaspoons grated lemon zest

Advance Preparation: To prepare the marinade, combine all the ingredients in a small bowl and mix well. (The marinade can be covered and refrigerated for up to 8 hours before using.) Within 1 hour of cooking, place the salmon in a shallow baking dish and cover with the marinade. Cover and refrigerate, turning occasionally, for 1 hour.

Last-Minute Cooking: Prepare a medium fire in a charcoal grill or preheat a gas grill to medium. When hot, place the salmon, skin side down, on the grill rack and close the lid. Cook for 8 minutes without lifting the lid, then check for doneness. If the flesh does not flake with slight pressure from a fork, cover the barbecue for another 3 minutes, then check again. Continue checking every 3 minutes until done. Slide a spatula between the flesh and skin, and transfer to a serving platter. Sprinkle with the orange and lemon zests and serve at once.

Menu suggestions: rice pilaf (page 101); salad greens with a dressing from page 106.

Brian Streeter, the chef at Cakebread Cellars, showed me this wonderfully simple way to cook salmon. Cut into serving-size portions and baked in a very low oven, all the interior moisture and the intensely beautiful color of the fish are retained.

Roast Salmon with Thai Coconut Sauce

SERVES 4

Sauce
2 tablespoons finely minced ginger
1 cup unsweetened coconut milk
2 tablespoons white wine
1 teaspoon cornstarch
2 teaspoons Asian chile sauce
1 teaspoon curry powder
$\frac{1}{2}$ teaspoon salt
$\frac{1}{4}$ cup chopped fresh cilantro sprigs or basil

2 pounds fresh salmon fillet (not the tail section), skinned and pin bones removed
1 lime, cut into wedges

Advance Preparation: To prepare the sauce, in a small bowl, combine all the ingredients, reserving 2 tablespoons of the cilantro, and mix well. Cut the salmon into 8-ounce pieces. (All of the ingredients can be covered and refrigerated for up to 8 hours before using.)

Last-Minute Cooking: Preheat the oven to 300°F. Line a baking sheet with aluminum foil. Place the salmon on the prepared baking sheet, making sure that the pieces do not touch. Place in the oven and bake for 18 to 20 minutes, until the fish just begins to flake with slight pressure from a fork. Stir the sauce to dissolve any cornstarch that may have settled to the bottom and pour into a saucepan over medium-high heat. Bring to a fast boil for 30 seconds. Taste and adjust the seasoning if necessary. Transfer the salmon to warmed dinner plates and spoon the sauce over. Garnish with the reserved cilantro and serve at once, accompanied by the lime wedges.

Menu suggestions: store-bought pecan wild rice mix; avocado and arugula salad.

This is one of our favorite marinades for broiled salmon and other firm-fleshed fish. It's got a great contrast of flavors that lingers long after the last bite. We have also enjoyed substituting a good oil and vinegar salad dressing, enlivened with a squeeze of fresh lemon or lime juice, a dash of hot sauce, and a few cloves of minced garlic. Before broiling the salmon, please review the broiling techniques described on pages 16 to 17.

Asian Broiled Salmon

SERVES 4

Asian Marinade
$\frac{1}{4}$ cup dry sherry or white wine
2 tablespoons thin soy sauce
2 tablespoons oyster sauce
2 tablespoons freshly squeezed lemon juice
2 tablespoons dark sesame oil
$\frac{1}{2}$ teaspoon freshly ground black pepper
2 tablespoons minced fresh chives
$\frac{1}{4}$ cup finely minced ginger

2 pounds fresh salmon fillet, skinned and pin bones removed
4 lemon wedges

Advance Preparation: To prepare the marinade, combine all the ingredients in a small bowl and mix well. (The marinade can be covered and refrigerated for up to 8 hours before using.) Place the salmon in a shallow baking dish and cover with the marinade. Cover and marinate, turning occasionally, for 15 minutes.

Last-Minute Cooking: Preheat the oven to 500°F. Place a rack 4 inches from the heating element. Line a shallow baking dish with aluminum foil. Transfer the salmon to the prepared baking dish and pour the marinade into a small saucepan. Turn the oven to broil, place the salmon in the oven, and close the door. Broil for about 5 minutes, until golden. If the salmon is not fully cooked (the flesh should flake with slight pressure from a fork), return the oven to bake at 500°F. Continue cooking with the oven door closed, until done. Transfer to warmed dinner plates. Bring the marinade in the saucepan to a boil for 1 minute over high heat. Spoon the marinade over the salmon and serve at once, accompanied by lemon wedges.

Menu suggestions: oven-roasted new potatoes (page 101); yellow tomato salad.

Crisp Pan-Fried Trout

SERVES 4

5 vine-ripe tomatoes, seeded and chopped (about 3 cups)
½ cup chicken broth
¼ cup chopped fresh basil
3 cloves garlic, minced
2 teaspoons plus ¼ cup cornstarch
¾ teaspoon salt
½ teaspoon crushed red pepper flakes
4 (8-ounce) fresh trouts, bone-in or boned
¼ cup olive oil
⅓ cup freshly grated imported Parmesan cheese

Advance Preparation: In a bowl, combine the tomatoes, broth, basil, garlic, the 2 teaspoons cornstarch, salt, and pepper flakes and mix well. (The tomato mixture can be covered and refrigerated for up to 8 hours before cooking.)

Last-Minute Cooking: Lightly salt the trout on both sides, then rub with the ¼ cup cornstarch, shaking off any excess. Place a large heavy sauté pan over medium-high heat. When the pan is hot, add the oil. When the oil begins to smoke, add the trout, shaking the pan to prevent sticking. (If using boned trout, do not spread it open in the pan.) Fry, turning once, for about 3 minutes on each side for boned trout or about 4 minutes for bone-in. Regulate the heat so that the oil always sizzles but does not smoke. When the flesh just begins to flake with slight pressure from a fork, transfer the fish to a plate. Drain the oil out of the pan. Stir the tomato mixture, add to the pan, and bring to a boil. Return the trout to the pan and gently turn in the sauce. Transfer the fish to warmed dinner plates and spoon the sauce over. Sprinkle with the cheese and serve at once.

Menu suggestions: store-bought rice mix; boiled or steamed artichokes with mayonnaise dip.

This recipe is also excellent if you substitute fillet of sole, red snapper, sand dabs, or any other very thin fillet. Although this recipe calls for dusting the fish with cornstarch, you can substitute an equal amount of flour or bread crumbs following the method on page 25.

Pan-Fried Sole with Capers and Lemon

SERVES 4

1½ pounds fresh fillet of sole, cut into equal pieces
½ cup all-purpose flour
3 eggs, beaten
1 cup bread crumbs or Japanese bread crumbs (panko)
Salt
Freshly ground black pepper
2 tablespoons olive oil
2 tablespoons unsalted butter
3 tablespoons drained capers, rinsed
Juice of 2 lemons
¼ cup chopped fresh parsley

Advance Preparation: Lightly dust the fish on both sides with the flour, then dredge in the eggs. Evenly coat the fish with the bread crumbs, season with salt and pepper, and place on a wire rack. (The fish can be covered and refrigerated for up to 8 hours before cooking.)

Last-Minute Cooking: Place 2 large sauté pans over medium-high heat. When the pans are hot, add the oil and butter, dividing evenly. When the butter melts and begins to brown lightly, add the fish to the pans in a single layer. Cook, turning once, for about 1 minute on each side, until the fish just begins to flake with slight pressure from a fork. Transfer to warmed dinner plates. Sprinkle on the capers and lemon juice, garnish with parsley, and season with salt and pepper. Serve at once.

Menu suggestions: garlic bread (page 103); avocado and spinach salad with bacon, oil, and vinegar dressing.

Breading fish: Coat both sides of the fish with the flour, shaking off any excess. Dip the fish into the beaten eggs. Coat the fish on both sides with the bread crumbs.

For barbecued fish, use any of the following choices interchangeably: halibut steaks and fillets, salmon steaks and fillets, shark, swordfish, tuna, and mahi mahi. Place fragile fish fillets such as bass, catfish, snapper, and tilapia on a layer of aluminum foil.

Swordfish with Lemon-Ginger Butter

SERVES 4

½ cup unsalted butter, at room temperature
3 tablespoons minced ginger
2 tablespoons minced fresh chives
2 tablespoons minced fresh mint
1 tablespoon grated lemon zest
1 teaspoon salt
1 teaspoon freshly ground black pepper
1 teaspoon Asian chile sauce
Juice of 1 lemon
4 (8-ounce) fresh swordfish steaks, each 1 inch thick
4 lemon wedges

Advance Preparation: Combine the butter, ginger, chives, mint, lemon zest, salt, pepper, and chile sauce in a food processor and process until evenly blended. Transfer to a small bowl. (The seasoned butter can be covered and refrigerated for up to 8 hours before using.)

Last-Minute Cooking: Prepare a medium fire in a charcoal grill or preheat a gas grill to medium. Season the swordfish with salt and pepper on both sides. Pour the lemon juice over the swordfish. When the grill is hot, brush the grill rack with oil, and place the fish on the rack. Grill, turning once, for 3 to 4 minutes on each side, until it just loses its raw color in the center (cut into a piece to check). During the last 1 minute of cooking, spread the seasoned butter evenly over the fish. Transfer to warmed dinner plates and serve at once, accompanied by the lemon wedges.

Menu suggestions: store-bought couscous mix; salad greens with lime-honey dressing (page 106).

When pan-frying fish, it's important that the pan is hot enough to maintain a consistent sizzling sound during cooking, but not so hot that the fish begins to burn. Better to turn the fish over frequently than wait too long and have a shock! If the swordfish steaks are more than 1 inch thick, cover the pan during frying to create a mini-oven and speed the cooking time.

Swordfish with Green Peppercorn Crust

SERVES 4

¼ to ⅓ cup drained green peppercorns bottled in brine
2 tablespoons grated lemon zest
4 (8-ounce) fresh swordfish steaks, each 1 inch thick
½ teaspoon salt
1 cup finely ground dried bread crumbs
¼ cup olive oil
2 cloves garlic, finely minced
1 lemon, cut into wedges
1½ cups store-bought tropical fruit or tomato salsa (optional)

Advance Preparation: Rinse the peppercorns, then finely mince in an electric mini-chopper (this works better than using a mortar and pestle). Rub the peppercorns and lemon zest on both sides of the swordfish. (The fish can be covered and refrigerated for up to 8 hours before cooking.)

Last-Minute Cooking: Sprinkle the salt on both sides of the swordfish. Dust both sides with bread crumbs, shaking off any excess. Place 2 large sauté pans over medium heat. When the pans are hot, add the oil, dividing evenly. When the oil is hot, add the garlic, again dividing evenly. Sauté for 15 seconds, until aromatic. Add the swordfish and decrease the heat to low. Cook, turning once, for 3 to 4 minutes on each side, until the fish is golden and just loses its raw color in the center (cut into a piece to check). Transfer to warmed dinner plates or a serving platter, and serve at once, accompanied by the lemon wedges and salsa.

Menu suggestions: mashed potatoes (page 101); store-bought coleslaw.

Broiled Halibut with Terrific Tartar Sauce

SERVES 4

Terrific Tartar Sauce
½ cup mayonnaise
2 tablespoons chopped pickles or whole capers
2 tablespoons chopped fresh basil, parsley, mint, or cilantro sprigs
1 tablespoon finely minced ginger
1 tablespoon freshly squeezed lemon or lime juice
1 teaspoon Worcestershire Sauce
1 teaspoon your favorite hot sauce

¼ cup freshly squeezed lemon or lime juice
¼ cup white wine
¼ cup thin soy sauce
2 tablespoons extra virgin olive oil
2 pounds fresh halibut, salmon, swordfish, shark, or catfish fillets

Advance Preparation: To prepare the tartar sauce, in small bowl, combine all the ingredients and mix well. In another small bowl, combine the lemon juice, wine, soy sauce, and oil and mix well. (All the ingredients can be covered and refrigerated for up to 8 hours before using.) Place the halibut in a shallow baking dish and cover with the lemon juice–soy sauce mixture. Cover and marinate, turning occasionally, for 15 to 30 minutes.

Last-Minute Cooking: Preheat the oven to 500°F. Place a rack 4 inches from the heating element. Line a shallow baking dish with aluminum foil. Transfer the halibut to the prepared baking dish and pour the marinade into a small bowl. Turn the oven to broil, place the halibut in the oven, and close the door. Broil for about 5 minutes, until golden. Brush with the marinade, and continue to broil for 1 minute. If the halibut is not fully cooked (the flesh should flake with slight pressure from a fork), return the oven to bake at 500°F. Continue cooking with the oven door closed, until done. Transfer to warmed dinner plates and serve immediately, accompanied by the tartar sauce.

Menu suggestions: pasta and tomato sauce; salad greens with a dressing from page 106.

Whenever possible, buy fresh fish rather than frozen—its taste and texture are better. You can judge freshness by appearance: very fresh fish has a beautiful glossy sheen that is entirely absent from fish beyond its prime or frozen fish. If you aren't cooking the fish the day it's purchased, it should be wrapped in plastic, placed on a plate, covered with a bag of ice, and refrigerated. The ice will keep the fish very cold without freezing its surface. If you still have not used fish two days after purchase, it should be cooked and then refrigerated. Cooked fish keeps perfectly for two days and is great in salads and sandwiches.

Ahi Tuna with Ginger-Basil Butter Sauce

If you don't like raw to medium-rare tuna, substitute another fish such as swordfish or shark in this recipe, and cook it until the flesh flakes with slight pressure from a fork. Tuna is so lean that cooking it to medium creates a much too dry texture. We always purchase sashimi-grade tuna, which is a rich deep red.

SERVES 4

2 tablespoons white sesame seeds
2 pounds fresh tuna steaks, each 1 inch thick
2 teaspoons plus ⅛ teaspoon freshly ground black pepper
⅓ cup dry white wine
3 tablespoons white wine vinegar
1 tablespoon finely minced ginger
1 teaspoon grated lemon zest
3 tablespoons minced fresh basil leaves, mint leaves, or cilantro sprigs
½ teaspoon salt
¼ cup thin soy sauce
6 tablespoons unsalted butter, cut into 6 pieces, at room temperature
3 tablespoons heavy cream
1 lemon, cut into wedges

Advance Preparation: Place the sesame seeds in a dry sauté pan over medium heat and toast for about 2 minutes, until golden. Cut the tuna into 1-inch-thick strips and place in a shallow baking dish. Rub the tuna with the sesame seeds and the 2 teaspoons pepper. To prepare the sauce, in a saucepan, combine the wine, vinegar, and ginger over high heat. Bring to boil for about 1 minute, until reduced to ¼ cup. Combine the lemon zest, basil, salt, and the ⅛ teaspoon pepper. (All the ingredients can be covered and refrigerated for up to 8 hours before grilling.)

Last-Minute Cooking: Coat all sides of the tuna with the soy sauce and marinate for 10 minutes. Prepare a hot fire in a charcoal grill or preheat a gas grill to high. When hot, brush the grill rack with oil, and place the tuna on the rack. Grill, turning once, for about 15 seconds on each side, until seared. Transfer to warmed dinner plates. Bring the wine mixture to a rapid boil over high heat. Add the butter and cream all at once and beat vigorously with a whisk. When just a few lumps of butter remain, remove the saucepan from the heat and stir in the lemon zest mixture. Spoon the sauce around the tuna. Serve at once, accompanied by the lemon wedges.

Menu suggestions: sourdough rolls; sliced tomato salad drizzled with extra virgin olive oil, balsamic vinegar, salt, and freshly ground black pepper.

There are several ways to know when fish is properly cooked: Apply slight pressure with a fork—the flesh should just begin to flake. Or, press a Chinese chopstick (not the pointed Japanese chopsticks) into the surface—the chopstick should sink easily into the fish. Or, if the fish is at least an inch thick, insert an instant-read meat thermometer horizontally into the center of the fish—the temperature should read 130°F.

Turning fish over while sautéing: *Place one hand across the top of the fish (this uncooked side will still be cool), slide a spatula under the fish, and then, still supporting the uncooked side of the fish with your hand, carefully turn it over.*

Sautéed Red Snapper with Pesto Sauce

SERVES 4

Pesto Sauce
4 cloves garlic
½ cup fresh basil leaves
¼ cup freshly grated imported Parmesan cheese
¼ cup pine nuts, raw or toasted
¾ teaspoon salt
¼ teaspoon freshly ground black pepper
¼ cup extra virgin olive oil

¼ cup heavy cream
½ cup chicken broth
2 pounds fresh red snapper fillets
Salt
Freshly ground black pepper
½ cup all-purpose flour
¼ cup olive oil

Advance Preparation: To prepare the pesto sauce, mince the garlic in a food processor. Add the basil and mince again. Add the cheese, pine nuts, salt, and pepper and process. With the machine running, slowly pour the olive oil down the feed tube and process until uniformly smooth. Transfer to a small bowl. (The pesto can be covered and refrigerated for up to 8 hours before using.)

Last-Minute Cooking: In a small bowl, combine the cream and broth and mix well. Place 2 large sauté pans over medium-high heat. Season the fish with salt and pepper, then lightly coat with flour on both sides, shaking off any excess. Add the oil to the pans, dividing evenly. When the oil is hot, add the fish and sauté, turning once, for 3 to 4 minutes on each side, until golden and just beginning to flake with slight pressure from a fork. Transfer to warmed dinner plates. Return 1 sauté pan to medium-high heat. Add the cream-broth mixture and the pesto sauce to the pan. Bring to a rapid boil for about 45 seconds, until reduced and thickened. Spoon the sauce over the fish. Grind some black pepper over the fish and serve at once.

Menu suggestions: oven-roasted new potatoes (page 101); carrot salad.

Simple Shellfish Entrées

Sautéed Shrimp with Cantonese Glaze

SERVES 4

Sauce

⅓ cup chicken broth
3 tablespoons oyster sauce
1 tablespoon finely minced ginger
1 tablespoon grated or minced lemon zest
2 teaspoons cornstarch
1 teaspoon sugar
½ teaspoon freshly ground black pepper
¼ cup chopped cilantro sprigs

1½ pounds raw medium or large shrimp
2 tablespoons peanut or safflower oil

Advance Preparation: To prepare the sauce, in a small bowl, combine all the ingredients and mix well. Shell, devein, and butterfly the shrimp as shown here. (The sauce and the shrimp can be covered and refrigerated for up to 8 hours before cooking.)

Last-Minute Cooking: Place a large sauté pan over high heat. When hot, add the oil. When the oil begins to smoke, add the shrimp. Stir and toss for about 90 seconds, until the shrimp turn pink. Stir the sauce and add it to the pan. Cook for 1 to 2 minutes, until the sauce thickens and the shrimp are white in the center (cut into one to check). Transfer to warmed dinner plates and serve at once.

Menu suggestions: Chinese-style steamed rice (page 100); steamed or microwaved zucchini with melted butter, salt, and pepper.

Shelling shrimp: *Using your thumb, loosen the shell from the underside of the fattest part of the shrimp. Slide your thumb along the underside to loosen the entire edge of the shell. Holding the shell, gently rotate the shrimp to remove the shell.*

Removing shrimp tails: *Hold the tail shell and pull gently. The shell should come away, leaving the tail meat intact.*

Butterflying shrimp: *Place the shrimp on a cutting board, curved side up. Cut deeply along the ridge without going all the way through. Rinse out the vein and pat dry with paper towels.*

Barbecued Caribbean Shrimp

SERVES 4

1½ pounds raw large shrimp
8 (6-inch) bamboo skewers
½ cup puréed fresh pineapple
½ cup pineapple juice
½ cup orange marmalade
¼ cup thin soy sauce
4 cloves garlic, finely minced
1 to 4 serrano chiles, finely minced including seeds
¼ cup chopped cilantro sprigs or mint

Advance Preparation: Shell and devein the shrimp as shown on page 31. Place on the skewers as shown on page 35, dividing equally. In a bowl, combine the puréed pineapple, pineapple juice, marmalade, soy sauce, garlic, chiles, and cilantro and mix well. (All of the ingredients can be covered and refrigerated for up to 8 hours before grilling.)

Last-Minute Cooking: Within 15 minutes of cooking, coat the shrimp with half of the pineapple mixture, reserving the remainder for serving. Prepare a medium fire in a charcoal grill or preheat a gas grill to medium. When hot, brush the grill rack with oil and place a double layer of aluminum foil on the rack to protect the exposed ends of the skewers. Place the skewers on the rack and grill, turning once, for 2 minutes on each side, until the shrimp are white in the center (cut into one to check). Transfer the skewers to warmed dinner plates. Spoon the reserved pineapple mixture over the shrimp and serve at once.

Menu suggestions: deli-bought rice dish; fresh asparagus grilled alongside the shrimp.

This barbecue sauce is also delicious with fish, chicken, and pork. Because the pineapple in the sauce is so acidic, it will turn food into mush with even brief marinating. Therefore, don't spoon the sauce over the food until just before it goes on the grill. You can buy pineapple already cut into cubes in the produce section of most markets. There should be enough juice in the bottom of the container to complete this recipe.

Thai Sautéed Shrimp

We think that spending a little extra money for large shrimp (15 per pound) is well worth it. Shelling and deveining are much quicker for large shrimp than smaller ones. No matter what size the shrimp, it's important to butterfly them before sautéing. Not only does this create even cooking, but the soft, fleshy interior absorbs the sauce far better than the surface of the shrimp does.

SERVES 4

1½ pounds raw large shrimp
2 tablespoons peanut or safflower oil
4 cloves garlic, minced
2 to 3 small fresh hot chiles, such as serranos, minced
⅓ cup chicken broth
2 teaspoons grated or minced lime zest
Juice of 1 lime
1 tablespoon Thai or Vietnamese fish sauce or thin soy sauce
1 tablespoon light brown sugar
1 teaspoon cornstarch
¼ cup fresh mint or basil leaves, shredded or chopped

Advance Preparation: Shell, devein, and butterfly the shrimp as shown on page 31. In a small bowl, combine the oil, garlic, and chiles and mix well. In a separate small bowl, combine the broth, lime zest, lime juice, fish sauce, brown sugar, and cornstarch and mix well. (All of the ingredients can be covered and refrigerated for up to 8 hours before cooking.)

Last-Minute Cooking: Place a large sauté pan over high heat. When hot, add the oil mixture and sauté for 15 seconds, until aromatic. Add the shrimp and sauté for about 2 minutes, until pink. Stir the lime juice mixture and add it to the pan. Taste and adjust the seasoning, if necessary, then stir in the mint. Transfer to warmed dinner plates and serve at once.

Menu suggestions: warm flour tortillas; deli-bought gazpacho soup.

Skewered Shrimp with Peanut Glaze

SERVES 4

1½ pounds raw medium or large shrimp
8 (6-inch) bamboo skewers
¼ cup freshly squeezed lime or lemon juice
¼ cup white wine or dry sherry
2 tablespoons peanut or safflower oil
½ cup natural-style chunky peanut butter
1 cup freshly squeezed orange juice
2 tablespoons honey
2 tablespoons wine vinegar or freshly squeezed lime or lemon juice
2 teaspoons your favorite hot sauce
2 cloves garlic, finely minced
¼ cup minced green onion, mint leaves, or cilantro sprigs

Advance Preparation: Shell, devein, and butterfly the shrimp as shown on page 31. Place on skewers as shown here, dividing equally. In a small bowl, combine the lime juice, wine, and oil and mix well. (The shrimp and the lime juice mixture can be covered and refrigerated for up to 8 hours.) In a separate bowl, combine the peanut butter, orange juice, honey, vinegar, hot sauce, garlic, and 2 tablespoons of the green onion and whisk well. (The peanut butter mixture can be kept at room temperature for up to 8 hours before using.)

Last-Minute Cooking: Prepare a medium fire in a charcoal grill or preheat a gas grill to medium. When hot, brush the shrimp on both sides with the lime juice mixture. Brush the grill rack with oil and place a double layer of aluminum foil on the rack to protect the exposed ends of the skewers. Place the skewers on the rack and brush again with the lime juice mixture. Grill, turning once, for 2 minutes on each side, until white in the center (cut into one to check). Spoon the peanut butter sauce onto warmed dinner plates. (Extra sauce can be refrigerated for up to 5 days.) Remove the skewers from the grill and place on top of the sauce. Sprinkle with the remaining 2 tablespoons green onion and serve at once.

Menu suggestions: warm corn tortillas and shredded iceberg lettuce for wrapping; matchstick-cut jicama tossed with your favorite oil and vinegar dressing.

Because it is so perishable, most markets sell shrimp that has been frozen and thawed. Ask at the market and buy only shrimp that has been thawed that day. We prefer to buy frozen shrimp in 4-pound boxes from Asian markets. It is less expensive than at American markets and we can control the defrosting. To defrost, run cold water over one end of the block of shrimp. Once you've defrosted as much as you need, return the rest of the frozen shrimp to the freezer.

Skewering shrimp: Line up the shrimp so that they are curved around each other. Insert two parallel skewers into the shrimp. When barbecuing, protect the exposed skewer ends with a double layer of aluminum foil.

If you don't cook shrimp the day you buy it, store it on ice: Place the shrimp in a colander within a bowl. Cover with plastic wrap, then add handfuls of ice cubes and refrigerate. Be sure to cook the shrimp the next night.

Lemon Shrimp

SERVES 4

¼ cup white sesame seeds
1½ pounds raw medium or large shrimp
¼ cup freshly squeezed lemon juice
¼ cup chicken broth
¼ cup sugar
1½ teaspoons cornstarch
1 teaspoon Asian chile sauce
½ teaspoon salt
2 tablespoons finely minced ginger
¼ cup chopped fresh parsley

Advance Preparation: Place the sesame seeds in a dry sauté pan over medium heat and toast for about 2 minutes, until golden. Shell, devein, and butterfly the shrimp as shown on page 31 (leave the tails on if desired). In a bowl, combine the lemon juice, broth, sugar, cornstarch, chile sauce, salt, and ginger and mix well. (The shrimp and the lemon juice mixture can be covered and refrigerated for up to 8 hours before cooking.)

Last-Minute Cooking: In a large pot, bring 4 quarts of water to a rapid boil and lightly salt. Add the shrimp and stir continuously for about 30 seconds, until pink. Remove 1 shrimp and cut into it. If it's not white in the interior, return to the pot and continue cooking. Repeat this test every 15 seconds until the shrimp are done. Drain in a colander. Immediately return the pot to high heat. Stir the lemon juice mixture to dissolve any cornstarch that may have settled, pour it into the pot, and bring to a boil. Return the shrimp to the pot, add the sesame seeds, and stir well. Transfer to warmed dinner plates, sprinkle with parsley, and serve at once.

Menu suggestions: Chinese-style steamed rice (page 100); steamed asparagus sprinkled with soy sauce, a few drops of dark sesame oil, and freshly ground black pepper.

Removing sea scallop muscles:
using your fingers, pull away the
small muscle from the side of large
scallops.

Scallops with Chiles and Mint

SERVES 4

1½ *pounds fresh sea scallops*
1 *tablespoon finely minced ginger*
3 *cloves garlic, finely minced*
2 *serrano chiles, minced including seeds*
¼ *cup shredded fresh mint*
Juice of 2 limes
3 *tablespoons honey*
2 *tablespoons Thai or Vietnamese fish sauce*
8 (6-inch) *bamboo skewers*

Advance Preparation: Remove the secondary muscle from the scallops as shown here. In a small bowl, combine the ginger, garlic, chiles, mint, lime juice, honey, and fish sauce and mix well. (The scallops and the lime juice mixture can be covered and refrigerated for up to 8 hours before grilling.)

Last-Minute Cooking: Place the scallops in a shallow baking dish. Reserve half of the lime juice mixture, spoon the remainder over the scallops, and marinate for 15 minutes. Place the scallops on the skewers as shown for shrimp on page 35, dividing equally. Prepare a medium fire in a charcoal grill or preheat a gas grill to medium. When hot, brush the grill rack with oil and place a double layer of aluminum foil on the rack to protect the exposed ends of the skewers. Place the scallops on the rack and grill, turning once and brushing with some of the reserved marinade, for about 2 minutes, until opaque and still slightly soft. Transfer to warmed dinner plates. Spoon on the remaining reserved lime juice mixture. Serve at once.

Menu suggestions: garlic bread (page 103); deli-bought Cobb salad.

For the best flavor and texture, scallops should always be bought fresh. Frozen and thawed scallops expel a milky liquid during cooking, which affects both the tenderness and flavor of the scallops. At the market, fresh scallops will be sitting in a clear liquid and will have a pleasant smell. Thawed scallops will be surrounded by a milky liquid and will have no odor until they begin to spoil.

Spicy Tex-Chinese Scallops

SERVES 4

2 *tablespoons minced chipotle chiles in adobo sauce*
3 *cloves garlic, minced*
¼ *cup chicken broth*
2 *tablespoons freshly squeezed lime juice*
2 *tablespoons oyster sauce*
1 *tablespoon light brown sugar*
2 *teaspoons cornstarch*
1 *teaspoon ground cumin*
2 *tablespoons corn or safflower oil*
1½ *pounds fresh bay scallops*
¼ *cup chopped cilantro sprigs*

Advance Preparation: In a small bowl, combine the chiles, garlic, broth, lime juice, oyster sauce, sugar, cornstarch, and cumin and mix well. (The mixture can be covered and refrigerated for up to 8 hours before cooking.)

Last-Minute Cooking: Place a large sauté pan over high heat. When very hot, add the oil. When the oil just begins to smoke, add the scallops. Stir and toss for about 1 minute, until the scallops firm slightly and begin to turn white. Discard any moisture that has accumulated in the pan. Add the chile mixture to the pan and stir and toss for about 30 seconds, until the sauce forms a glaze on the scallops. Stir in the cilantro. Transfer to warmed dinner plates and serve at once.

Menu suggestions: roasted peeled yams rubbed with butter and brown sugar; papaya salad with oil and vinegar dressing.

There are two cardinal rules for sautéing scallops: the pan must be very hot and it must not be overcrowded. If the pan is too cool or too crowded, a large amount of moisture will quickly leach from the scallops, producing a milky broth. If this occurs, discard the liquid before adding a sauce, or the results will be a bland disappointment.

Spicy Mussels with Roasted Red Peppers

SERVES 4

3 pounds small black mussels, tightly closed
½ cup homemade or store-bought roasted red bell peppers, chopped
¼ cup chopped fresh cilantro, mint, or basil
2 cloves garlic, finely minced
3 tablespoons Japanese rice vinegar
2 tablespoons thin soy sauce
1 tablespoon sugar
1 tablespoon dark sesame oil
1 tablespoon peanut or safflower oil
2 teaspoons Asian chile sauce
1 teaspoon cornstarch

Advance Preparation: Scrub the mussels and remove the beard as shown on page 41. In a small bowl, combine the bell peppers, cilantro, garlic, vinegar, soy sauce, sugar, sesame oil, peanut oil, chile sauce, and cornstarch and mix well. (The mussels and the sauce can be covered and refrigerated for up to 8 hours before cooking.)

Last-Minute Cooking: Place a colander in a bowl. In a large saucepan, bring 2 cups of water to a rapid boil over high heat. Add the mussels and cover the pot tightly. When steam begins to escape from the lid after about 3 minutes, remove the lid and stir the mussels. As soon as the mussels open, drain them in the colander (the captured mussel broth can be frozen for later use in flavoring sauces and soups). Return the empty saucepan to high heat. Stir the red pepper sauce, add it to the pan, and bring to a boil. Return the mussels to the saucepan and stir well. Transfer to 4 warmed soup bowls and serve at once.

Menu suggestions: oven-roasted new potatoes (page 101); microwaved zucchini with melted butter, salt, and freshly ground black pepper

Roasting bell peppers: *Place the peppers on the grill rack or over a high gas stovetop flame and cook until blackened on all sides. Place in a plastic bag, seal, and let sweat for 10 minutes. Peel, stem, and seed the peppers, then chop as needed.*

Steamed Mussels in Thick Coconut Sauce

SERVES 4

3 pounds small black mussels, tightly closed

3 tablespoons finely minced ginger

6 tablespoons chopped fresh basil leaves, mint leaves, or cilantro sprigs

2 cups unsweetened coconut milk (see sidebar)

3 tablespoons thin soy sauce

Juice of 2 limes

1 tablespoon Asian chile sauce

2 teaspoons cornstarch

Advance Preparation: Scrub the mussels and remove the beard as shown here. In a small bowl, combine the ginger, basil, coconut milk, soy sauce, lime juice, chile sauce, and cornstarch and mix well. (The mussels and the coconut milk mixture can be covered and refrigerated for up to 8 hours before cooking.)

Last-Minute Cooking: Place a colander in a bowl. In a large saucepan, bring 2 cups of water to a rapid boil over high heat. Add the mussels and cover the pot tightly. When steam begins to escape from the lid after about 3 minutes, remove the lid and stir the mussels. As soon as the mussels open, drain them in the colander (the captured mussel broth can be frozen for later use in flavoring sauces and soups). Return the empty saucepan to high heat. Stir the coconut sauce, add it to the pan, and bring to a boil. Return the mussels to the saucepan and stir well. Transfer to 4 warmed soup bowls and serve at once.

Menu suggestions: warm baguette; arugula salad with toasted cashews.

At the top of unshaken cans of coconut milk, a layer of thick coconut milk (sometimes called coconut cream) forms. For this recipe, spoon off all the thick coconut milk from the top and then add the thinner coconut milk from the bottom to yield the 2 cups needed.

Removing mussel beards: *using your fingers, pull away the beard from between the shells.*

Steamed Clams with Rich Meat Glaze

Always buy tightly closed mussels and clams without cracked shells. As soon as possible after purchase, place the shellfish in a small colander within a bowl, cover with a wet dishtowel, add a mound of ice on top, and refrigerate. Stored in this manner, the mussels or clams will maintain a perfect state of freshness for 2 days. Mussels and clams can be used interchangeably in any of these recipes.

We're very specific about the type of clams we eat, preferring manila. Occasionally markets sell cockles, another excellent small clam. Other varieties are inferior: steamer clams are filled with sand, while littleneck and cherrystone clams open unevenly and have tough textures.

SERVES 4

3 pounds manila clams, tightly closed
3 cloves garlic, finely minced
¼ pound ground beef, lamb, pork, or meatloaf mix
1½ cups tomato purée or diced tomatoes, drained of all liquid
3 tablespoons chopped fresh basil or oregano
½ teaspoon grated orange zest
2 teaspoons your favorite hot sauce
2 teaspoons cornstarch
½ teaspoon salt
2 tablespoons extra virgin olive oil
¼ cup freshly grated imported Parmesan cheese

Advance Preparation: Scrub the clams. In a bowl, combine the garlic and ground beef and mix well. In a separate bowl, combine the tomato purée, basil, orange zest, hot sauce, cornstarch, and salt and mix well. (All the ingredients can be covered and refrigerated for up to 8 hours before cooking.)

Last-Minute Cooking: Place a colander in a bowl. In a large saucepan, bring 2 cups of water to a rapid boil over high heat. Add the clams and cover the pot tightly. Boil for about 3 minutes, until the clams open. Drain in the colander, capturing the cooking liquid in the bowl. Return the empty saucepan to high heat and add the olive oil. When the oil is hot, add the ground beef. Cook, pressing the meat against the sides of the pan, for about 2 minutes, until it breaks into individual clumps and loses its pink color. Stir the tomato mixture, add it to the pan, and bring to a rapid boil. Pass ½ cup of the reserved cooking liquid through a fine-mesh sieve and add to the pan. Return the clams to the pan and stir to combine evenly. Stir in the cheese, or sprinkle on top after serving. Transfer to 4 warmed soup bowls and serve at once.

Menu suggestions: warm deli-bought vegetarian ravioli; tomato-avocado salad.

Flavorful Chicken and Game Hens

Perfect Pan-Fried Chicken

This recipe uses a technique that yields perfect results with minimal mess: after the chicken is browned in a sauté pan over high heat, it's covered and "roasted" over low heat until fully cooked. Cooked in its own little oven, the chicken acquires a satisfyingly intense flavor.

SERVES 4

4 to 6 fresh skin-on chicken breast halves, bone-in; or 2 to 3 game hens, halved
Salt
Freshly ground black pepper
2 teaspoons dried oregano, thyme, or basil
¹/₂ cup all-purpose flour or dried bread crumbs
¹/₄ cup olive oil
1 cup freshly squeezed orange juice
¹/₄ cup chopped fresh parsley, basil, or oregano

Last-Minute Cooking: Place a sauté pan large enough to hold all the chicken in a single layer over medium-high heat. Season the chicken with salt, pepper, and oregano and dust with flour, shaking off any excess. When the pan is hot, add the oil. When the oil is hot, add the chicken, skin side down. Cook, turning once, for about 5 minutes total, until golden. Cover the pan and decrease the heat to low. Continue cooking for 14 to 18 minutes, until the internal temperature registers 160°F on an instant-read meat thermometer. The juices should run clear when the meat is pierced with a fork. Transfer the chicken to warmed dinner plates. Add the orange juice to the pan and bring to a rapid boil. Boil for about 2 minutes, until reduced by half, and then spoon over the chicken. Sprinkle the parsley on the chicken and serve at once.

Menu suggestions: pasta variation (page 103); salad greens with ginger-citrus dressing (page 106).

Pan-Fried Chicken with Bananas

SERVES 4

¼ cup orange marmalade

2 tablespoons finely minced ginger

1 clove garlic, minced

1 cup chicken broth or orange juice

½ teaspoon freshly ground nutmeg, plus additional for serving

½ teaspoon salt

1 teaspoon Asian chile sauce

4 firm bananas

4 to 6 fresh boneless, skin-on chicken breast halves; or 2 to 3 game hens, halved

Freshly ground black pepper

½ cup all-purpose flour

3 tablespoons olive oil

1 tablespoon unsalted butter

¼ cup chopped fresh parsley or cilantro sprigs

Advance Preparation: In a small bowl, combine the marmalade, ginger, garlic, broth, nutmeg, salt, and chile sauce and mix well. (The mixture can be covered and refrigerated for up to 8 hours before cooking.)

Last-Minute Cooking: Peel and then cut the bananas in half lengthwise. Preheat the oven to 325°F. Place an ovenproof sauté pan large enough to hold all the chicken in a single layer over medium-high heat. Season the chicken with salt and pepper and dust with flour, shaking off any excess. When the pan is hot, add the oil and butter. When the butter is melted, add the chicken. Cook, turning once, for about 5 minutes total, until browned. Transfer the chicken to a plate and wipe out any excess oil from the pan. Return the chicken to the pan and add the marmalade mixture. Bring to a simmer, then cover the pan and transfer to the oven. Continue cooking for 8 to 10 minutes for chicken and 14 to 18 minutes for game hens until the internal temperature registers 155°F on an instant-read meat thermometer. The juices should run clear when the meat is pierced with a fork. Transfer the chicken to warmed dinner plates, leaving the sauce in the pan. Place the pan on the stovetop over medium-high heat, add the bananas, and bring to a boil. Boil for about 2 minutes, until thickened. Arrange the bananas next to the chicken and spoon on the sauce. Sprinkle with parsley, grate nutmeg over each serving, and serve at once.

Menu suggestions: rice pilaf (page 101).

Cutting chicken into pieces:
Using poultry shears, remove the legs at the thigh joint. Separate the drumsticks and thighs. Cut away and discard the backbone. Separate the breasts. Cut off the wings if you wish.

Barbecued Game Hens with Lemon Glaze

SERVES 4

Lemon Glaze

½ cup freshly squeezed lemon juice

6 tablespoons sugar

¼ cup chicken broth

2 tablespoons thin soy sauce

2 teaspoons cornstarch

½ teaspoon your favorite hot sauce or Asian chile sauce

½ teaspoon salt

½ cup white wine or dry sherry

½ cup freshly squeezed lemon juice

½ cup thin soy sauce

4 cloves garlic, minced

2 to 3 game hens, halved; or 2 (3-pound) fresh frying chickens, cut into pieces; or 4 to 6 skin-on
    chicken breast halves, bone-in

¼ cup chopped fresh chives, parsley leaves, or cilantro sprigs

Advance Preparation: To prepare the glaze, in a saucepan, combine all the ingredients and mix well. In a small bowl, combine the wine, lemon juice, soy sauce, and garlic and mix well. Reserve ½ cup of the wine mixture for basting. Place the game hens in a shallow dish, add the remaining wine mixture, and turn to coat evenly. Cover and refrigerate the game hens for at least 10 minutes and up to 8 hours, turning occasionally. (The glaze and reserved wine mixture can be covered and refrigerated for up to 8 hours before using.)

Last-Minute Cooking: Prepare a medium fire in a charcoal grill or preheat a gas grill to medium. When hot, brush the grill rack with oil and place the game hens on the rack, discarding the marinade. Grill, turning and basting occasionally with the reserved wine mixture, for 20 to 25 minutes total cooking time, until the internal temperature registers 160°F on an instant-read meat thermometer for game hens and chicken breasts and 170°F for chicken legs. The juices should run clear when the meat is pierced with a fork. Alternatively, roast the game hens in a 425°F oven. Transfer the game hens to warmed dinner plates. Place the lemon glaze over medium-high heat and bring to a boil. Pour the glaze over the game hens, sprinkle on the chives, and serve at once.

Menu suggestions: roasted yams and parsnips; papaya salad.

Chicken and game hens always benefit from long marinating because the time allows the meat to fully absorb the marinade's flavors. However, marinating for longer than 8 hours is unnecessary as the flavor does not noticeably improve past that point. Chicken should be marinated in the refrigerator in a nonreactive dish (not aluminum or iron) and turned every few hours.

Splitting game hens: *Using poultry shears, cut the game hens in half through the breast and backbone. Cut away and discard the backbone if you wish.*

This is a perfect recipe to serve very judgmental, calorie-counting, and dour guests, who will be horrified by this zany technique. They'll never return! The beer cans hold the chicken upright on the grill, acting as vertical chicken roasters. Using this unusual method, the heat rotates evenly around the chickens while the fat from the wings and neck bastes the breasts, making them extremely succulent. An added advantage is that during cooking, the seasoned beer boils and the moisture and flavors seep directly into the meat.

Placing chicken on beer can: *Carefully push the chicken onto the can. Transfer the chicken to the barbecue rack and stand upright, using the can and chicken legs to form a tripod.*

Barbecued Chicken on Beer Thrones

SERVES 4

2 (3-pound) fresh frying chickens, or 3 to 4 game hens
2 cups Lemon-Soy Marinade (page 49) or your favorite marinade
2 to 4 cans beer
2 tablespoons grated orange zest
6 cloves garlic, chopped
2 tablespoons chopped fresh rosemary

Advance Preparation: Place the chicken in a shallow baking dish and add 1½ cups of the the marinade. Turn the chicken to coat evenly. Cover and refrigerate for at least 10 minutes and up to 8 hours. Using 2 cans of beer for chicken or 4 cans for game hens, discard (or drink) half of each beer. Divide the orange zest, garlic, and rosemary evenly among the cans. (The beer can be covered and refrigerated for up to 8 hours before using.)

Last-Minute Cooking: Prepare a medium fire in a charcoal grill or preheat a gas grill to medium. When hot, place the beer cans upright on a flat surface and gently push the chickens over the cans so that the birds are upright (this process is easier when another person helps). Carefully transfer to the barbecue and cover the grill. Grill, basting occasionally with the remaining ½ cup marinade, for about 30 minutes, until the internal temperature registers 170°F on an instant-read meat thermometer for chicken (insert the thermometer in the thighs) and 160°F for game hens. The juices should run clear when the meat is pierced with a fork. Alternatively, roast the chicken in a 425°F oven. Cut the chicken into serving pieces or cut the game hens in half. Transfer to warmed dinner plates and serve at once.

Menu suggestions: corn bread muffins; tomato-basil salad.

Chicken with Herb-Mustard Marinade

SERVES 4

5 cloves garlic, finely minced
2 to 4 tablespoons minced fresh sage, basil, rosemary, or cilantro sprigs
2 tablespoons grated lemon zest
½ cup Dijon or honey mustard
½ cup white wine or dry sherry
½ cup extra virgin olive oil
¼ cup freshly squeezed lemon juice
2 teaspoons salt
2 teaspoons crushed red pepper flakes or your favorite hot sauce
2 (3-pound) fresh frying chickens, cut into pieces; or 4 to 6 skin-on chicken breast halves, bone-in or boneless; or 3 to 4 game hens, halved

Advance Preparation: In a bowl, combine the garlic, sage, lemon zest, mustard, wine, oil, lemon juice, salt, and pepper flakes and mix well. Reserve ½ cup of the marinade for basting. Place the chicken in a shallow baking dish, add the remaining marinade, and turn to coat evenly. Cover and refrigerate for at least 10 minutes and up to 8 hours, turning occasionally.

Last-Minute Cooking: Prepare a medium fire in a charcoal grill or preheat a gas grill to medium. When hot, brush the grill rack with oil and place the chicken on the rack, discarding the marinade. Grill, turning and basting occasionally with the reserved marinade, for 20 to 25 minutes total cooking time, until the internal temperature registers 160°F on an instant-read meat thermometer for chicken breasts and game hens and 170°F for chicken legs. The juices should run clear when the meat is pierced with a fork. Alternatively, roast the chicken in a 425°F oven. Transfer to warmed dinner plates and serve at once.

Menu suggestions: potato salad; grilled summer squash stuffed with bread crumbs and goat cheese.

Flavor-Packed Chicken

SERVES 4

Lemon-Soy Marinade
½ cup freshly squeezed lemon or orange juice
½ cup thin soy sauce
¼ cup honey
¼ cup extra virgin olive oil
1 tablespoon your favorite hot sauce
8 cloves garlic, minced
½ cup chopped fresh sage, basil, cilantro sprigs, or mint

2 (3-pound) fresh frying chickens, halved; or 4 game hens, halved

Advance Preparation: To prepare the marinade, in a small bowl, combine all the ingredients and mix well. Starting along the chicken breast, gently push your fingers between the skin and meat, loosening the skin across the breasts and legs. Reserve ½ cup of the marinade for basting. Pour ¼ cup of the marinade under the skin of the breasts and legs. Place the chicken in a small roasting pan, pour the remaining marinade over, and turn to coat evenly. Cover and refrigerate for at least 10 minutes and up to 8 hours, turning occasionally.

Last-Minute Cooking: Prepare a medium fire in a charcoal grill or preheat a gas grill to medium. When hot, brush the grill rack with oil and place the chicken on the rack, discarding the marinade. Grill, turning and basting occasionally with the reserved marinade, for about 25 minutes total cooking time, until the internal temperature registers 170°F on an instant-read meat thermometer for chicken (insert the thermometer in the thighs) and 160°F for game hens. The juices should run clear when the meat is pierced with a fork. Alternatively, roast the chicken in a 425°F oven. Transfer to warmed dinner plates and serve at once.

Menu suggestions: store-bought quick-cook risotto; spinach salad with blue cheese dressing (page 106).

Let the technique described in this recipe be your guide for using other seasonings under the skin of chicken or game hens. Any poultry or seafood marinade is great when placed between the skin and meat, and slathered on the outside of the skin. Use this method only when barbecuing whole or halved chickens; if you loosen the skin on smaller pieces, it will fall off during grilling and the meat will toughen.

Placing seasoning under poultry skin: Gently push your index finger under the breast skin, loosening the skin across the breasts and legs. Place seasonings between the meat and skin.

Spicy Chinese Barbecued Chicken

SERVES 4

4 cloves garlic, finely minced
2 tablespoons finely minced ginger
2 green onions, white and green parts, minced
¼ cup chopped cilantro sprigs
½ cup freshly squeezed orange juice
¼ cup hoisin sauce
¼ cup oyster sauce
2 tablespoons dark sesame oil
1 tablespoon Asian chile sauce
2 (3-pound) fresh frying chickens, cut into pieces; or 4 to 6 skin-on
  chicken breast halves, bone-in or boneless; or 3 to 4 game hens, halved

Advance Preparation: In a bowl, combine the garlic, ginger, onions, cilantro, orange juice, hoisin sauce, oyster sauce, sesame oil, and chile sauce and mix well. Reserve ½ cup of the marinade for basting. Place the chicken in a shallow baking dish, add the remaining marinade, and turn to coat evenly. Cover and refrigerate for at least 10 minutes and up to 8 hours, turning occasionally.

Last-Minute Cooking: Prepare a medium fire in a charcoal grill or preheat a gas grill to medium. When hot, brush the grill rack with oil and place the chicken on the rack, discarding the marinade. Grill, turning and basting occasionally with the reserved marinade, for 20 to 25 minutes total cooking time, until the internal temperature registers 170°F on an instant-read meat thermometer for chicken (insert the thermometer in the legs) and 160°F for game hens. The juices should run clear when the meat is pierced with a fork. Alternatively, roast the chicken in a 425°F oven. Transfer to warmed dinner plates and serve at once.

Menu suggestions: Chinese restaurant fried rice; Chinese chicken salad without the chicken.

New Orleans Chicken

In this recipe, bone-in and skin-on chicken breasts are simmered with rice and a spicy New Orleans blend of seasonings. The breast bone distributes the heat evenly, and both the bone and the skin prevent the meat from becoming overcooked while the rice is cooking. Use a heavy pot such as enamelware cast iron to achieve even cooking and to keep the food warm once it's cooked. For food safety reasons, this dish should be served within 30 minutes of cooking, and it doesn't reheat well.

SERVES 4

1 cup chopped andouille sausage or spicy salami
1½ cups long-grain white rice (not minute or converted), rinsed
4 cloves garlic, finely minced
2 tablespoons chopped fresh oregano
2 bay leaves
3 cups chicken broth
2 tablespoons Worcestershire sauce
1 teaspoon salt
1 teaspoon ground cayenne pepper
4 to 6 fresh bone-in, skin-on chicken breast halves; or 2 to 3 game hens, halved
Freshly ground black pepper
½ cup all-purpose flour
¼ cup olive oil
½ cup chopped fresh parsley

Advance Preparation: In a bowl, combine the sausage and rice and mix well. In another bowl, combine the garlic, oregano, bay leaves, broth, Worcestershire sauce, salt, and cayenne and mix well. (All the ingredients can be covered and refrigerated for up to 8 hours before cooking.)

Last-Minute Cooking: Place a large high-sided sauté pan or a soup pot over medium-high heat. Season the chicken with salt and pepper. Dust on both sides with the flour, shaking off any excess. When the pan is hot, add the oil. When the oil is hot, add the chicken. Cook, turning once, for about 5 minutes on each side, until browned. Add the sausage and rice and pour in the broth mixture. Bring to a boil, then cover and decrease the heat to achieve a simmer. Cook for about 20 minutes, until the rice is fully cooked and the internal temperature of the chicken registers 160°F on an instant-read meat thermometer. The juices should run clear when the meat is pierced with a fork. Transfer to warmed dinner plates, sprinkle with the parsley, and serve at once.

Menu suggestions: iceberg lettuce salad with blue cheese dressing (page 106).

Chicken Breasts with Tomato-Basil Glaze

SERVES 4

4 vine-ripe tomatoes, chopped including seeds
¼ cup chopped fresh basil
3 cloves garlic, minced
½ cup chicken broth, cream, or half-and-half
2 tablespoons balsamic vinegar
½ teaspoon salt
¼ teaspoon freshly ground black pepper
4 to 6 fresh skin-on chicken breast halves, bone-in or boned; or 2 to 3 game hens, halved
½ cup all-purpose flour
¼ cup olive oil
¼ cup freshly grated imported Parmesan cheese

Advance Preparation: In a bowl, combine the tomatoes, basil, garlic, broth, vinegar, salt, and pepper and mix well. (The mixture can be covered and refrigerated for up to 8 hours before cooking.)

Last-Minute Cooking: Place a sauté pan large enough to hold the chicken in a single layer over medium-high heat. Lightly season the chicken with salt and pepper. Dust both sides with the flour, shaking off any excess. When the pan is hot, add the oil. When the oil is hot, add the chicken. Cook, turning once, for about 5 minutes on each side, until browned. Remove the chicken from the pan and wipe out any excess oil. Return the pan to medium-high heat, add the chicken, skin side up, and spoon in the tomato mixture. Bring to a low boil, cover, and decrease the heat to achieve a simmer. Cook for about 8 minutes for boneless chicken, and 14 minutes for bone-in chicken, until the internal temperature registers 160°F on an instant-read meat thermometer. The juices should run clear when the meat is pierced with a fork. Transfer to warmed dinner plates. Sprinkle with the cheese and serve at once.

Menu suggestions: pasta variation (page 103); endive salad with walnuts and olives.

Prior to simmering chicken in a sauce, brown it first to seal the exterior and lock in the moisture. Without this browning step, juices will leach from the meat, leaving it dry and tough.

Spicy Wok Chicken with Asparagus

SERVES 2 TO 4

1/3 cup freshly squeezed orange juice or chicken broth

2 tablespoons oyster sauce

2 tablespoons hoisin sauce

1 tablespoon dark sesame oil

2 teaspoons cornstarch

2 teaspoons Asian chile sauce

1 pound boneless, skinless chicken breast or thigh meat

1 pound asparagus

3 cloves garlic, finely minced

3 tablespoons peanut or safflower oil

Advance Preparation: In a small bowl, combine the orange juice, oyster sauce, 1 tablespoon of the hoisin sauce, sesame oil, cornstarch, and chile sauce and mix well. Cut the chicken into 1-inch cubes. Place the chicken in a bowl, add the remaining 1 tablespoon hoisin sauce and 3 tablespoons of the orange juice mixture and stir to coat evenly. Cover and refrigerate for at least 10 minutes and up to 8 hours. Snap off and discard the tough asparagus ends. Cut the asparagus on a sharp diagonal into 2-inch lengths and combine with the garlic in a bowl. (The asparagus and the orange juice mixture can be covered and refrigerated for up to 8 hours before cooking.)

Last-Minute Cooking: Place a wok over high heat. When the wok is hot, add 1½ tablespoons of the peanut oil and roll around the sides of the wok. When the oil is hot, add the chicken. Stir and toss for about 2 minutes, until it loses its pink color but is still slightly undercooked. Transfer the chicken to a plate. Return the wok to high heat and add the remaining 1½ tablespoons peanut oil. When the oil is hot, add the asparagus. Stir-fry for about 1 minute, until bright green. Pour in the orange juice mixture and return the chicken to the wok. Stir and toss for about 1 minute, until the sauce glazes the food. Transfer to warmed dinner plates or serve family style. Serve at once.

Menu suggestions: Chinese-style steamed rice (page 100); Chinese restaurant won ton soup.

This recipe uses chicken breasts or thigh meat. The breast meat is easier to cut but thighs will be richer tasting and more tender. If using thigh meat, be sure to get boned and skinned thighs. You'll need about 6 thighs to yield 1 pound of meat.

Great Pork and Veal Recipes

Pork tenderloin is the only pork cut that we recommend using in stir-fry recipes. It's easy to cut against the grain into paper-thin slices, and the meat is far juicier than pork chops.

Removing pork silver skin:
Make a shallow cut along the length of the silver skin. Turn the meat so that the cut section of silver skin is against the cutting board. Hold the edge of the silver skin with your fingers while gently scraping it away from the meat with a knife. The tenderloin will roll as you cut away the silver skin.

Wok Pork with Roasted Peppers and Chiles

SERVES 2 TO 4

1 pound fresh pork tenderloin, silver skin removed
3 cloves garlic, finely minced
1 tablespoon grated lemon zest
1/4 cup tapenade (see page 12)
3 tablespoons olive oil
1/2 cup roasted red bell peppers, chopped (page 39)
1/4 cup chopped fresh basil
1/2 teaspoon crushed red pepper flakes
1/2 teaspoon salt
Juice of 1/2 lemon

Advance Preparation: Cut the pork crosswise into 1/8-inch slices. Cut the slices in half crosswise. Place the pork in a bowl and add the garlic, lemon zest, tapenade, and 2 tablespoons of the oil and stir to coat evenly. Cover and refrigerate for at least 10 minutes and up to 8 hours.

Last-Minute Cooking: Place a wok or heavy sauté pan over high heat. When the wok is hot, add the remaining 1 tablespoon oil and roll around the sides of the wok. When the oil is hot, add the pork. Stir and toss for about 1 minute, until the pork is no longer pink on the outside. Add the bell peppers, basil, pepper flakes, and salt. Continue cooking for 2 minutes, until the pork loses all of its raw color. Add lemon juice to taste. Transfer to warmed dinner plates and serve at once.

Menu suggestions: Charred corn tortillas (page 89) brushed with Dijon mustard or hoisin sauce; steamed or microwaved broccoli.

Tangerine Pork with Bok Choy

SERVES 2 TO 3

Tangerine Sauce
2 tablespoons finely minced ginger
2 tablespoons chopped fresh basil leaves or cilantro sprigs
1 tablespoon grated tangerine or orange zest
⅓ cup unsweetened coconut milk
Juice of 1 tangerine or orange
2 tablespoons oyster sauce
1 teaspoon Asian chile sauce
1 teaspoon cornstarch

5 stalks bok choy
1 pound fresh pork tenderloin, silver skin removed (page 56)
3 tablespoons peanut or safflower oil

Advance Preparation: To prepare the sauce, in a small bowl, combine all the ingredients and mix well. Cut the bok choy into triangle-shaped pieces as shown here. (The bok choy can be covered and refrigerated for up to 8 hours before cooking.) Cut the pork crosswise into ⅛-inch slices. Cut the slices in half crosswise and place in a bowl. Add ¼ cup of the sauce to the pork and stir to coat evenly. Cover and refrigerate the pork for at least 10 minutes and up to 8 hours.

Last-Minute Cooking: Place a wok over high heat. When the wok is hot, add 1½ tablespoons of the oil. When the oil is hot, add the pork. Stir and toss for about 1 minute, until the pork is no longer pink on the outside. Transfer to a plate and return the wok to high heat. Add the remaining 1½ tablespoons oil. When the oil is hot, add the bok choy and stir-fry for about 1 minute, until the color brightens. Stir the sauce, add it to the wok, and return the pork to the wok. Stir and toss for about 1 minute, until the sauce glazes the food. Transfer to warmed dinner plates and serve at once.

Menu suggestions: garlic bread (page 103); salad greens with lime-honey dressing (page 106).

Triangle-cutting bok choy:
Separate the bok choy leaves. Cut a triangle from the stalk of a leaf. Turn the leaf over, then cut on a sharp diagonal to form a second triangle. Return the leaf to its original position and repeat cutting and rotating. Repeat with remaining leaves.

While this recipe uses a goat cheese–dried fruit stuffing, any stuffing, from sausage to your favorite bread stuffing, would work with this technique. If the stuffing requires a preliminary cooking, it must be chilled thoroughly in the refrigerator before being packed into the pork chop pockets.

Cutting a pocket in pork chops: *Using a thin knife, cut deeply into the side of the chop. Carefully cut along the length of the chop, opening as large a pocket as possible.*

Barbecued Stuffed Double-Thick Pork Chops

SERVES 4

4 (1½-inch-thick) bone-in fresh pork chops or veal chops
5 ounces soft goat cheese
½ cup chopped mixed dried fruit, such as apricots, apples, pears, and peaches
3 cloves garlic, finely minced
2 tablespoons chopped fresh oregano
½ teaspoon salt
¼ teaspoon crushed red pepper flakes
1 cup your favorite barbecue sauce
Store-bought or homemade applesauce, for accompaniment

Advance Preparation: Cut a horizontal pocket in each chop as shown here. In a bowl, combine the goat cheese, fruit, garlic, oregano, salt, and pepper flakes and mix well. Stuff the cheese mixture into the pork chop pockets, dividing evenly. Brush the chops on both sides with the barbecue sauce. (The pork chops can be covered and refrigerated for up to 8 hours before grilling.)

Last-Minute Cooking: Prepare a medium fire in a charcoal grill or preheat a gas grill to medium. When hot, brush the grill rack with oil and place the chops on the rack. Cook for about 2 minutes on each side, until seared. Move the meat over indirect heat if using a charcoal grill or decrease the heat to medium-low if using a gas grill. Brush on additional barbecue sauce during cooking. Cover the barbecue and cook, turning every 5 minutes, for about 15 minutes, until the meat registers 145°F on an instant-read meat thermometer. The meat should still be slightly pink in the center. Transfer to warmed dinner plates and serve at once, accompanied by applesauce.

Menu suggestions: baked potatoes; salad greens with oil and vinegar dressing.

When grilling pork and veal, "low and slow" is always better than "hot and quick." Once the meat has been seared at medium heat so that the outside has turned light brown, decrease the heat and complete the cooking in a 275 to 325°F environment. With this technique, the meat will cook evenly to whatever degree of doneness you desire.

Barbecued Pork with Garlic-Rosemary Rub

SERVES 4

3 tablespoons chopped fresh rosemary

4 cloves garlic, finely minced

1 tablespoon grated lemon zest

¼ cup freshly squeezed lemon juice

¼ cup Dijon mustard

¼ cup thin soy sauce

¼ cup freshly squeezed orange juice

2 tablespoons extra virgin olive oil

2 tablespoons honey

1 teaspoon crushed red pepper flakes

2 (12- to 14-ounce) fresh pork tenderloins, silver skin removed (page 56);
*   or 4 (1- to 2-inch-thick) bone-in pork chops or veal chops*

Advance Preparation: In a bowl, combine the rosemary, garlic, lemon zest, lemon juice, mustard, soy sauce, orange juice, oil, honey, and pepper flakes and mix well. Reserve ½ cup of the marinade for basting. Place the pork in a shallow baking dish, add the remaining marinade, and turn to coat evenly. Cover and refrigerate for at least 10 minutes and up to 8 hours, turning occasionally.

Last-Minute Cooking: Prepare a medium fire in a charcoal grill or preheat a gas grill to medium. When hot, brush the grill rack with oil and place the pork on the rack, discarding the marinade. Cook for about 2 minutes on each side, until seared. Move the meat over indirect heat if using a charcoal grill or decrease the heat to medium-low if using a gas grill. Cover the barbecue and cook, turning and basting with the reserved marinade every 5 minutes, for about 15 minutes, until the meat registers 145°F on an instant-read meat thermometer. The meat should still be slightly pink in the center. Transfer the pork tenderloin to a cutting board and let rest for 5 minutes, then slice and place on warmed dinner plates. Serve at once.

Menu suggestions: mashed potatoes (page 101); tomato salad.

Pork Chops with Charred Tomatoes

SERVES 4

5 vine-ripe tomatoes
2 tablespoons plus ½ teaspoon sugar
¼ cup peanut or safflower oil
3 cloves garlic, finely minced
2 tablespoons oyster sauce
1 teaspoon Asian chile sauce or your favorite hot sauce
3 tablespoons chopped fresh oregano
4 (1- to 2-inch-thick) bone-in pork chops or veal chops
Salt
Freshly ground black pepper
½ cup all-purpose flour

Advance Preparation: Prepare a very hot fire in a charcoal grill or preheat a gas grill to high. Char and chop the tomatoes as shown on page 85. Place a small sauté pan over medium heat. When hot, add 1 tablespoon of the oil. When the oil is hot, add the garlic and sauté for about 1 minute, until it begins to brown. Immediately add the tomatoes, the ½ teaspoon sugar, oyster sauce, chile sauce, and oregano and bring to a simmer. (The tomato mixture can be covered and refrigerated for up to 8 hours before using.)

Last-Minute Cooking: Season the pork chops with salt and pepper. Lightly dust on both sides with flour, shaking off any excess. Place a large sauté pan over medium-high heat. When the pan is hot, add the remaining 3 tablespoons oil. When the oil just begins to smoke, add the chops. Cook, turning once, for 2 minutes on each side, until browned. Add the tomato mixture and bring to a boil. Cover the pan and decrease the heat to achieve the lowest possible simmer. Cook for 5 to 10 minutes, until the meat registers 145°F on an instant-read meat thermometer. The meat should still be slightly pink in the center. Transfer the chops to warmed dinner plates. Spoon the sauce over and serve at once.

Menu suggestions: warm sourdough rolls; deli-bought Cobb salad.

We're huge fans of charred tomatoes. We prepare them by sprinkling thick slices of tomato on both sides with sugar, then placing them over a very hot fire or on a very hot cast-iron grill pan. The sugar caramelizes on the surface while the interior moisture cooks away, concentrating the flavor. Charred tomatoes make a great addition to salsa, tomato sauces, tomato soups, and to practically any sauce.

Chops with Blue Cheese, Chiles, and Walnuts

SERVES 4

¼ cup peanut or safflower oil
2 cloves garlic, minced
⅔ cup chicken broth
⅓ cup heavy cream
2 tablespoons oyster sauce
2 tablespoons freshly squeezed lemon juice
1 teaspoon cornstarch
1 teaspoon Asian chile sauce or your favorite hot sauce
4 (1- to 2-inch-thick) bone-in pork or veal chops
Salt
Freshly ground black pepper
½ cup all-purpose flour
¼ cup chopped fresh basil
2 ounces blue cheese, crumbled
¼ cup walnuts, toasted

Advance Preparation: Place a small sauté pan over medium heat. When hot, add 1 tablespoon of the oil. When the oil is hot, add the garlic and sauté for about 1 minute, until it begins to brown. Immediately stir in the broth, cream, oyster sauce, lemon juice, cornstarch and chile sauce. (The sauce can be covered and refrigerated for up to 8 hours before using.)

Last-Minute Cooking: Preheat the oven to 300°F. Season the pork chops with salt and pepper. Lightly dust on both sides with flour, shaking off any excess. Place a large sauté pan over medium-high heat. When the pan is hot, add the remaining 3 tablespoons oil. When the oil just begins to smoke, add the chops. Cook, turning once, for 2 minutes on each side, until browned. Transfer the pan to the oven. Cook for 10 to 12 minutes, until the meat registers 145°F on an instant-read meat thermometer. The meat should still be slightly pink in the center. Transfer the chops to warmed dinner plates. Return the pan to the stovetop over medium-high heat. Add the sauce and bring to a boil until thickened. Stir in the basil. Spoon the sauce over the chops, sprinkle on the cheese and nuts and serve at once.

Menu suggestions: egg noodles; arugula and bean sprout salad.

Never cook pork beyond a 160°F internal temperature or it will taste dry and its texture will be tough. We actually use 145°F as our benchmark, as the meat is perfectly cooked to a rosy color and juicy texture. Some people still have fears about trichinosis, but the bacterium that causes it was eliminated from pork products decades ago. Even if it were present, the bacterium is killed when the internal temperature reaches 140°F.

Roasted Pork Tenderloin with Sage and Fruit

SERVES 4

3 cups chicken broth
2½ cups mixed dried fruit, such as prunes, apricots, apples, pears, and peaches
4 cloves garlic, finely minced
¼ cup chopped fresh sage
½ teaspoon salt
½ teaspoon freshly ground black pepper
2 (12- to 14-ounce) fresh pork tenderloins, silver skin removed (page 56)

Advance Preparation: In a small saucepan, bring 2 cups of the broth to a simmer over medium-high heat. Pour into a bowl, add the dried fruit, garlic, sage, salt, and pepper and mix well. Allow to rest at room temperature for about 15 minutes, until the fruit plumps. (The fruit mixture can be covered and refrigerated for up to 8 hours before using.)

Last-Minute Cooking: Preheat the oven to 325°F. Prepare a medium fire in a charcoal grill or preheat a gas grill to medium. Season the pork with salt and pepper. Brush the grill rack with oil and place the pork on the rack. Cook, turning occasionally, for about 5 minutes, until all sides are seared. Alternatively, the meat can be seared on an indoor grill pan or in a heavy sauté pan. Transfer to a small roasting pan and add the fruit with its liquid. Place in the oven and cook, basting every 5 minutes, for about 15 minutes, until the internal temperature registers 145°F on an instant-read meat thermometer. The meat should still be slightly pink in the center. Transfer the meat to a cutting board and allow to rest for 5 minutes. Place the roasting pan on the stovetop over high heat. If all of the liquid has evaporated, add the remaining 1 cup broth. Bring the sauce to a boil until thickened. Slice the pork and place on warmed dinner plates. Spoon the sauce over and serve at once.

Menu suggestions: rice pilaf (page 101); mixed vegetable salad with oil and vinegar dressing.

Veal Scaloppine with Shiitakes

SERVES 4

½ pound fresh shiitake mushrooms
½ cup heavy cream
¼ cup white wine
2 tablespoons thin soy sauce
½ teaspoon Asian chile sauce or your favorite hot sauce
2 cloves garlic, minced
1½ pounds veal scaloppine or boneless, skinless chicken breasts,
    pounded to ⅛ to ¼ inch thick
Salt
Freshly ground black pepper
½ cup all-purpose flour
3 tablespoons olive oil
2 tablespoons chopped fresh cilantro sprigs, chives, or parsley

Pounding veal scaloppine:
Place the meat between two pieces of plastic wrap. Pound with a meat pounder, moving the pounder away from the center of the meat as you go to flatten and enlarge the scaloppine.

Advance Preparation: Cut off and discard the mushroom stems. Cut the mushroom caps into ¼-inch slices. In a small bowl, combine the cream, wine, soy sauce, chile sauce, and garlic and mix well. (All the ingredients can be covered and refrigerated for up to 8 hours before cooking.)

Last-Minute Cooking: Preheat the oven to 225°F. Place 2 large sauté pans over medium-high heat. Lightly season the veal with salt and pepper. Dust on both sides with the flour, shaking off any excess. When the pans are hot, add the oil, dividing evenly. When the oil is hot, add the veal in a single layer. (You may need to work in batches.) Cook, turning once, for 1 minute on each side, until lightly browned. Transfer to warmed dinner plates and place in the oven. Return 1 pan to high heat. Add the cream mixture and mushrooms and bring to a rapid boil for about 4 minutes, until thickened. Spoon the sauce over the veal, sprinkle with cilantro, and serve at once.

Menu suggestions: oven-roasted new potatoes (page 101); endive-watercress salad.

From the Range: Beef and Lamb

Barbecued Steaks with Balsamic-Soy Glaze

SERVES 4

4 (8-ounce) beef steaks, each 1 to 2 inches thick (listed in sidebar);
  or center-cut loin lamb chops; or boneless lamb leg meat
2 teaspoons freshly ground black pepper
$\frac{1}{2}$ cup Swedish or honey mustard
$\frac{1}{2}$ cup balsamic vinegar
$\frac{1}{2}$ cup red wine
$\frac{1}{4}$ cup dark or thin soy sauce
6 cloves garlic, finely minced
$\frac{1}{4}$ pound blue cheese, crumbled

Advance Preparation: Trim the fat from the steak. Rub both sides of the steak with the pepper. Place the steak in a shallow baking dish. In a bowl, combine the mustard, vinegar, wine, soy sauce, and garlic and mix well. Reserve $\frac{1}{2}$ cup of the marinade for basting. Pour the remaining marinade over the steak and turn to coat evenly. Cover and refrigerate for at least 10 minutes and up to 8 hours, turning occasionally.

Last-Minute Cooking: Prepare a medium fire in a charcoal grill or preheat a gas grill to medium. When hot, brush the grill rack with oil and place the steak on the rack, discarding the marinade. Grill, turning once and basting with the reserved marinade, for about 4 minutes on each side, until the meat registers 120°F on an instant-read meat thermometer for rare or 130°F for medium rare. Transfer to warmed dinner plates, sprinkle with the blue cheese, and serve at once.

Menu suggestions: baked potatoes; steamed carrots with butter and salt.

Following are the best (most tender) types of steaks to barbecue; they all should be 1 to 2 inches thick:

- beef tenderloin
- flank
- flat iron
- hanger
- New York strip
- porterhouse
- rib-eye
- T-bone

Steaks thinner than 1 inch are best barbecued over medium heat. The grill should be hot enough so that the steaks always make a sizzling sound. Steaks thicker than 1 inch will cook much more evenly through a preliminary searing and subsequent cooking over medium-low heat, similar to the technique discussed on page 60 for barbecuing pork tenderloin.

Texas Ranger Beef

SERVES 4

2 pounds beef tenderloin or other boneless steak (listed on page 67);
  or center-cut loin lamb chops; or boneless lamb leg meat
1/2 cup ketchup
1/4 cup minced canned chipotle chiles in adobo sauce
1/4 cup freshly squeezed orange juice
1/4 cup firmly packed brown sugar
1/4 cup wine vinegar
1/4 cup Worcestershire sauce
1 tablespoon chili powder
1 tablespoon ground coriander
6 cloves garlic, minced

Advance Preparation: Cut the tenderloin into 1- to 2-inch-thick steaks (or trim the fat from the steaks). Place the tenderloin in a shallow baking dish. In a bowl, combine the ketchup, chiles, orange juice, sugar, vinegar, Worcestershire sauce, chili powder, coriander, and garlic and mix well. Reserve 1/2 cup of the sauce for basting. Pour the remaining sauce over the meat and turn to coat evenly. Cover and refrigerate for at least 10 minutes and up to 8 hours, turning occasionally.

Last-Minute Cooking: Prepare a medium fire in a charcoal grill or preheat a gas grill to medium. When hot, brush the grill rack with oil and place the steak on the rack, discarding the marinade. Grill, turning once and brushing on the reserved sauce, for about 4 minutes on each side, until the meat registers 120°F on an instant-read meat thermometer for rare or 130°F for medium rare. Transfer to warmed dinner plates and serve at once.

Menu suggestions: roasted yams; Caesar salad.

The barbecue sauce in this recipe can be made in large amounts and refrigerated indefinitely. It's great on all types of barbecued or roasted meat.

Using a meat thermometer:
Insert the probe of an instant-read meat thermometer into the center point of the meat for boneless or close to the bone for bone-in.

Top sirloin, T-bone, or rib-eye steaks won't work for this recipe because they are difficult to cut against the grain into thin pieces, and thus often have a tough texture. On the other hand, beef tenderloin is easy to slice thinly and yields a tender result.

The special ingredient in this recipe is pomegranate syrup. Also called pomegranate molasses, this flavorful concoction is made of pomegranate juice, sugar, and lemon juice. Marvelously fruity and tart, it's great added to salad dressings; brushed across meats, seafood, and vegetables during grilling; drizzled on pancakes; and added to ice cream and sorbet. A good brand found in Middle Eastern stores and gourmet markets is Cortas, sold in 10-ounce bottles. Pomegranate syrup lasts indefinitely stored at room temperature.

Beef Satay with Curry Peanut Sauce

SERVES 4

2 pounds beef tenderloin or boneless lamb leg meat
12 (8-inch) bamboo skewers

Curry Peanut Sauce
½ cup natural-style peanut butter
½ cup freshly squeezed orange juice
¼ cup thin soy sauce
2 tablespoons honey
1 tablespoon curry powder
2 teaspoons Asian chile sauce
2 tablespoons chopped cilantro sprigs
3 cloves garlic, finely minced

Advance Preparation: Slice the meat into pieces ⅓ inch thick, 1 inch wide, and 4 inches long. Run the skewers through the meat so that just the ends of the skewers are visible. Place in a shallow dish. To prepare the sauce, in a bowl, combine all the ingredients and mix well. Coat the meat evenly with the sauce. Cover and refrigerate for at least 10 minutes and up to 8 hours, turning occasionally.

Last-Minute Cooking: Prepare a medium fire in a charcoal grill or preheat a gas grill to medium. Brush the grill rack with oil and place a double layer of aluminum foil on the rack to protect the exposed ends of the skewers. Place the skewers on the rack and grill, turning once, for about 45 seconds on each side for medium rare to medium. Transfer the skewers to warmed dinner plates or a platter. Serve at once.

Menu suggestions: warm tortillas for wrapping; spinach salad.

Kebabs with Pomegranate Essence

SERVES 4

2 pounds beef rib-eye, beef tenderloin, or boneless lamb leg meat

Pomegranate Essence
½ cup pomegranate syrup
½ cup freshly squeezed lemon juice
¼ cup extra virgin olive oil
4 cloves garlic, finely minced
2 tablespoons finely minced ginger
3 tablespoons minced fresh rosemary
1 teaspoon crushed red pepper flakes

Advance Preparation: Cut the meat into 1-inch cubes and place in a shallow baking dish. To prepare the essence, in a bowl, combine all the ingredients and mix well. Reserve $1/2$ cup of the essence for basting. Pour the remaining essence over the meat and turn to coat evenly. Cover and refrigerate for at least 10 minutes and up to 8 hours, turning occasionally. Thread the meat onto 8 (8-inch) metal skewers.

Last-Minute Cooking: Prepare a medium fire in a charcoal grill or preheat a gas grill to medium. When hot, brush the grill rack with oil and place the skewers on the rack, discarding the marinade. Grill, turning once and basting with the reserved essence, for about 1 minute on each side for medium rare. The meat should still be pink in the center. Transfer to warmed dinner plates and serve at once.

Menu suggestions: mashed potatoes (page 101); mango salad.

Best-Ever Asian Beef

SERVES 4

2 pounds beef tenderloin or other beef steaks (listed on page 67); or center-cut
   loin lamb chops; or boneless lamb leg meat
$3/4$ cup hoisin sauce
$1/2$ cup plum sauce
$1/4$ cup oyster sauce
$1/4$ cup dry sherry
2 tablespoons dark sesame oil
1 tablespoon Asian chile sauce
$1/2$ teaspoon five-spice powder
4 cloves garlic, finely minced
2 tablespoons finely minced ginger

Advance Preparation: Cut the tenderloin into 1-inch-thick steaks. Place the meat in a shallow baking dish. In a bowl, combine the hoisin sauce, plum sauce, oyster sauce, sherry, sesame oil, chile sauce, five-spice powder, garlic, and ginger and mix well. Reserve $1/2$ cup of the sauce for basting. Pour the remaining sauce over the meat and turn to coat evenly. Cover and refrigerate for at least 10 minutes and up to 8 hours, turning occasionally.

Last-Minute Cooking: Prepare a medium fire in a charcoal grill or preheat a gas grill to medium. Brush the grill rack with oil and place the meat on the rack, discarding the marinade. Grill, turning once and basting with the reserved sauce, for about 4 minutes on each side, until the meat registers 120°F on an instant-read meat thermometer for rare or 130°F for medium rare. Transfer to warmed dinner plates and serve at once.

Menu suggestions: Chinese restaurant fried rice and hot garlic eggplant.

The versatile Asian barbecue sauce in this recipe is our absolute favorite. We suggest you make it in large quantities to store in the refrigerator—it will keep indefinitely. The sauce is delicious when brushed on any meat or seafood being readied for the grill.

Follow these four essential rules to achieve the perfect burger: First, use freshly ground beef with a medium fat content. Meat that has been frozen or with a fat content lower than 22 percent will have a dry texture. Second, form the burgers by hand as shown on page 74, being careful not to overcompact. Machine-formed burgers are too heavy and dense. Third, for the perfect juiciness, don't cook burgers beyond medium. And fourth, serve burgers on the best available buns, or sliced and toasted sourdough bread.

SERVES 4

2 pounds ground beef, 22 percent fat
¼ cup chopped cilantro sprigs
4 cloves garlic, minced
2 to 3 serrano chiles, minced including seeds
1 cup shredded sharp Cheddar cheese
1 teaspoon ground cumin
½ teaspoon salt
4 hamburger buns
Vine-ripe tomatoes, sliced
Lettuce
Homemade or store-bought salsa
Homemade or store-bought guacamole

Advance Preparation: Place the beef in a bowl and add the cilantro, garlic, chiles, cheese, cumin, and salt. Using your hands, mix thoroughly. Form the mixture into 4 equal-sized balls, then flatten gently with your palm. (The patties can be covered and refrigerated for up to 8 hours before grilling.)

Last-Minute Cooking: Prepare a medium fire in a charcoal grill or preheat a gas grill to medium. When hot, brush the grill rack with oil and place the burgers on the rack. Grill, turning once, for about 3 minutes on each side for medium rare or to desired doneness. Alternatively, cook the hamburgers in a cast-iron skillet over medium heat, or broil them 4 inches from the heating element. While the hamburgers are cooking, toast the buns. Place the burgers on the buns and served immediately, accompanied by sliced tomatoes, lettuce, salsa, and guacamole.

Menu suggestions: corn and arugula salad; deli-bought soup.

Chinese Pine Nut Burgers

SERVES 4

1/2 cup pine nuts
2 pounds ground beef, 22 percent fat
1/4 cup oyster sauce
3 cloves garlic, finely minced
2 tablespoons very finely minced ginger
1 teaspoon finely minced orange zest
1 teaspoon Asian chile sauce
1/4 cup hoisin sauce
2 tablespoons water
4 hamburger buns
Vine-ripe tomatoes, sliced
Lettuce, mayonnaise, and ketchup

Advance Preparation: Preheat the oven to 325°F. Spread the pine nuts on a small baking sheet and toast for about 8 minutes, until golden. Place the beef in a bowl and add the oyster sauce, garlic, ginger, orange zest, chile sauce, and pine nuts. Using your hands, mix thoroughly. Form the mixture into 4 equal-sized balls, then flatten gently with your palm. In a small bowl, combine the hoisin sauce and water. (All the ingredients can be covered and refrigerated for up to 8 hours.)

Last-Minute Cooking: Prepare a medium fire in a charcoal grill or preheat a gas grill to medium. When hot, brush the grill rack with oil and place the burgers on the rack. Grill, turning once, for about 3 minutes on each side for medium rare or to desired doneness. Alternatively, cook the hamburgers in a cast-iron skillet over medium heat, or broil them 4 inches from the heating element. Brush the hoisin sauce mixture on the cooked burgers. While the hamburgers are cooking, toast the buns. Place the burgers on the buns and served immediately, accompanied by sliced tomatoes, lettuce, mayonnaise, and ketchup.

Menu suggestion: salad greens with ginger-citrus dressing (page 106).

Mediterranean Pesto Burgers

SERVES 4

2 pounds ground beef or lamb, 22 percent fat
1 cup crumbled feta cheese
1/4 cup tapenade (see page 12)
1/4 cup chopped fresh basil
1/2 teaspoon freshly ground black pepper
4 hamburger buns
1/2 cup homemade or store-bought pesto
Vine-ripe tomatoes, sliced
Lettuce and mayonnaise

Shaping hamburgers: *Form the ground beef into balls. Flatten the balls gently with your palm so as not to compact the meat too tightly. Smooth the ragged edges.*

When using a gas barbecue, you can improve the flavor of the meat by smoking wood chips in the grill. And since hamburgers cook quickly, there's no need to soak the chips. Just place about 2 cups of chips in the barbecue's smoking tray, or place them on a piece of aluminum foil at one end of the grill rack. Once the wood begins to smoke heavily, proceed with the cooking.

Advance Preparation: Place the beef in a bowl and add the feta cheese, tapenade, basil, and pepper. Using your hands, mix thoroughly. Form the mixture into 4 equal-sized balls, then flatten gently with your palm. (The patties can be covered and refrigerated for up to 8 hours before grilling.)

Last-Minute Cooking: Prepare a medium fire in a charcoal grill or preheat a gas grill to medium. When hot, brush the grill rack with oil and place the burgers on the rack. Grill, turning once, for about 3 minutes on each side for medium rare or to desired doneness. Alternatively, cook the hamburgers in a cast-iron skillet over medium heat, or broil them 4 inches from the heating element. While the hamburgers are cooking, toast the buns. As soon as the burgers are cooked, brush them with the pesto. Place the burgers on the buns and serve immediately, accompanied by sliced tomatoes, lettuce, and mayonnaise.

Menu suggestions: artichoke salad.

Dinner Salads with Beef Tenderloin

SERVES 2 TO 3

1 pound beef tenderloin, trimmed of fat
2 tablespoons freshly squeezed lime juice
2 tablespoons thin soy sauce
1 tablespoon honey
2 teaspoons Asian chile sauce
1/2 teaspoon freshly grated nutmeg
2 tablespoons finely minced ginger
2 cloves garlic, minced
1/4 cup minced green onion, fresh basil leaves, or cilantro sprigs
Salad fixings of your choice (page 106)
Salad dressing of your choice (page 106)
2 tablespoons peanut or safflower oil

Advance Preparation: Cut the meat against the grain into 1/8-inch slices. Cut the slices into 1-inch lengths. In a bowl, combine the lime juice, soy sauce, honey, chile sauce, nutmeg, ginger, garlic, and green onion and mix well. Add the meat and toss to coat evenly. Cover and refrigerate for at least 10 minutes and up to 8 hours.

Last-Minute Cooking: Prepare the salad fixings and toss with the dressing. Divide the salad evenly among dinner plates. Place a wok over high heat. When the wok is very hot, add the oil and roll around the sides of the wok. When the oil just begins to smoke, add the meat. Stir and toss for about 3 minutes, until the meat is no longer pink on the outside. Slide the meat on top of the salads, dividing evenly, and serve at once.

Menu suggestion: oven-baked crispy sourdough rolls.

One of our favorite quick dinners is to stir-fry thinly sliced beef tenderloin and slide it piping hot over dinner salads. For our salad, we combine lettuce greens, sliced button mushrooms, avocado, and toasted nuts, and then toss with an oil and vinegar dressing. Accompanied by warm dinner rolls or a baguette and glasses of wine, this makes a delicious work-night meal.

Cutting beef for stir-frying:
Trim the silver skin off the tenderloin (page 56). Cut across the grain into 1/8- to 1/4-inch slices. Cut the slices into 1-inch lengths.

Rack of Lamb with Spicy Juniper Berry Glaze

SERVES 4

2 (1-pound) racks of lamb, trimmed
2 tablespoons juniper berries or minced fresh rosemary
1 teaspoon freshly ground black pepper
3 cloves garlic, minced
1 tablespoon grated orange zest
¾ cup freshly squeezed orange juice
½ cup thin soy sauce
¼ cup extra virgin olive oil
2 tablespoons honey
2 teaspoons Asian chile sauce or your favorite hot sauce

Advance Preparation: Trim any excess fat from the lamb and place in a shallow baking dish. Crush the juniper berries using a mortar and pestle. Rub the juniper berries and the pepper over the lamb. In a bowl, combine the garlic, orange zest, orange juice, soy sauce, oil, honey, and chile sauce and mix well. Reserve ½ cup of the marinade for basting. Coat all sides of the lamb with the remaining marinade. Cover and refrigerate for at least 10 minutes and up to 8 hours.

Last-Minute Cooking: Prepare a medium fire in a charcoal grill or preheat a gas grill to medium. When hot, brush the grill rack with oil, place the lamb on the rack, and cover the barbecue. Cook, turning and basting occasionally with the reserved marinade, for about 15 minutes, until the meat registers 130°F on an instant-read meat thermometer for medium rare. The meat should still be very pink in the center. Alternatively, roast the lamb in a 425°F oven for about 20 minutes. Transfer the lamb to a cutting board and let rest for 5 minutes. Cut the racks into chops and divide among warmed dinner plates. Serve at once.

Menu suggestions: garlic mashed potatoes; endive-watercress salad with blue cheese.

Sold in the spice section of most markets, juniper berries have an intense cypress tree smell and taste that complements grilled lamb.

Trimming rack of lamb: *Pull and cut off the thick layer of fat covering the ribs. Trim away the silver skin, but don't over trim—it's not necessary to remove all the silver skin. Using a paring or boning knife, cut and scrape the fat, membrane, and meat off the bones.*

Pasta Entrées in Minutes

M eat and seafood choices for adding to the pasta recipes in this book:

- *¾ to 1½ pounds any cooked meat or seafood, leftover or store-bought. Preparation: cut into bite-size pieces.*
- *¾ to 1½ pounds boneless, skinless chicken breasts; beef or pork tenderloin; shelled and deveined shrimp; or bay and sea scallops. Preparation and cooking: cut into bite-size pieces, marinate (using a marinade such as the one on page 49), and then sauté while the pasta is cooking.*
- *¾ to 1½ pounds fresh link sausage. Preparation and cooking: sauté until cooked through, then cut crosswise into ½-inch slices.*
- *3 pounds mussels or manila clams. Preparation and cooking: debeard mussels and cook as described on page 41 while the pasta is cooking.*

Wild Mushroom Pasta

SERVES 4

¾ pound assorted fresh mushrooms such as button, cremini, shiitake, and chanterelle
½ cup chicken broth
½ cup heavy cream
½ teaspoon salt
½ teaspoon freshly ground black pepper
½ teaspoon sugar
8 ounces dried fusilli, farfalle, or your favorite pasta
¼ cup unsalted butter
4 cloves garlic, finely minced
¾ to 1½ pounds cooked meat or seafood (listed in sidebar)
¼ pound imported Parmesan cheese, freshly grated
½ cup chopped fresh parsley

Advance Preparation: If using shiitake mushrooms, cut off and discard the stems. Thinly slice all the mushrooms. In a bowl, combine the broth, cream, salt, pepper, and sugar and mix well. (All the ingredients can be covered and refrigerated for up to 8 hours before cooking.)

Last-Minute Cooking: In a pot, bring 5 quarts of water to a rapid boil over high heat. Lightly salt the water and add the pasta. Cook according to the package instructions for about 12 minutes, until tender. Drain the pasta in a colander and return the empty pot to high heat. Add the butter and garlic. When the butter melts, add the mushrooms. Sauté for about 4 minutes, until the mushrooms release their moisture. Add the meat or seafood and the cream mixture and bring to a rapid boil. Return the pasta to the pot and stir to combine evenly. Stir in the cheese. Transfer to warmed dinner plates, sprinkle with parsley, and serve at once.

Menu suggestion: Bibb lettuce and pecan salad with a dressing from page 106.

Pasta with Orange and Toasted Sesame Seeds

SERVES 4

Orange Sauce

½ cup chopped green onion or cilantro sprigs
¼ cup freshly squeezed orange juice
2 tablespoons unseasoned rice vinegar
2 tablespoons thin soy sauce
2 tablespoons light brown sugar
1 tablespoon dark sesame oil
2 teaspoons Asian chile sauce

2 tablespoons peanut or safflower oil
4 cloves garlic, minced
1 tablespoon grated orange zest
¼ cup white sesame seeds
8 ounces dried linguine, spaghetti, or your favorite pasta
¾ to 1½ pounds cooked meat or seafood (listed on page 78)

Advance Preparation: To prepare the sauce, in a small bowl, combine all the ingredients and mix well. In a separate small bowl, combine the oil, garlic, and orange zest and mix well. Place the sesame seeds in a dry sauté pan over medium heat and toast for about 2 minutes, until golden. (All the ingredients except the sesame seeds can be covered and refrigerated for up to 8 hours. Store the sesame seeds at room temperature.)

Last-Minute Cooking: In a pot, bring 5 quarts of water to a rapid boil over high heat. Lightly salt the water and add the pasta. Cook according to the package instructions for about 12 minutes, until tender. Drain the pasta in a colander and return the empty pot to high heat. Add the oil-garlic mixture and sauté for 15 seconds, until aromatic. Add the sauce and bring to a boil. Add the meat or seafood and return the pasta to the pot. Add the sesame seeds and stir to combine evenly. Transfer to warmed dinner plates and serve at once.

Menu suggestion: steamed broccoli with butter and salt.

All of the pasta recipes in this book can be enhanced with the addition of vegetables, following these guidelines:

- *The ratio of vegetables to pasta should be 4 cups vegetables to 8 ounces dried pasta.*
- *Choose a combination of vegetables that will cook in the same amount of time when cut to the same size: button and cremini mushrooms, summer squash, green onions, bell peppers, bok choy and cabbages, asparagus, snow peas, and sugar snap peas.*
- *Cut hard vegetables such as carrots, cauliflower, and broccoli into bite-sized pieces and microwave briefly until tender before adding to the pasta.*
- *For vegetarian pasta entrées, drain the pasta, then add 2 tablespoons olive or vegetable oil to the hot pasta pot and sauté the vegetables. When tender, return the pasta to the pot and add any sauce.*

Toasting sesame seeds: *Place the sesame seeds in a dry sauté pan over medium heat. Stir or shake for about 2 minutes, until golden. Immediately tip out of the pan. The toasted seeds can be stored at room temperature for up to 4 months, or can be frozen indefinitely.*

Pasta with Chinese Pesto

Making Chinese pesto: *Place all the ingredients in a blender. Blend until smooth, cover, and refrigerate for up to 8 hours. Alternatively, combine all the ingredients in the blender but do not blend until just before cooking. Can be stored unblended in the refrigerator for up to 24 hours.*

SERVES 4

3 tablespoons white sesame seeds
2 cups firmly packed spinach leaves
1/4 cup firmly packed cilantro sprigs
1/4 cup firmly packed fresh basil leaves
1/4 cup firmly packed fresh mint leaves
4 cloves garlic, chopped
2 tablespoons minced ginger
1/2 cup chicken broth or orange juice
3 tablespoons thin soy sauce
2 tablespoons wine vinegar
2 tablespoons dark sesame oil
1 teaspoon hoisin sauce
1 teaspoon sugar
1 1/2 teaspoons Asian chile sauce
1/2 teaspoon salt
8 ounces dried fusilli, pappardelle, or your favorite pasta
3/4 to 1 1/2 pounds cooked seafood or meat (listed on page 78)

Advance Preparation: Place the sesame seeds in a dry sauté pan over medium heat and toast for about 2 minutes, until golden. In a blender, combine the spinach, cilantro, basil, mint, garlic, ginger, broth, soy sauce, vinegar, sesame oil, hoisin sauce, sugar, chile sauce, and salt and process until liquefied. (The sauce can be covered and refrigerated for up to 8 hours before using.)

Last-Minute Cooking: In a pot, bring 5 quarts of water to a rapid boil over high heat. Lightly salt the water and add the pasta. Cook according to the package instructions for about 12 minutes, until tender. Drain the pasta in a colander and return the empty pot to medium-high heat. Add the seafood or meat and stir for about 1 minute, until warmed. Return the pasta to the pot and add the pesto sauce. Stir to combine evenly. Transfer to warmed dinner plates, sprinkle with the sesame seeds, and serve at once.

Menu suggestion: salad greens with a dressing from page 106.

Curry, used in a variety of Southeast Asian cuisines, is defined as a combination of spices ground into a powder or blended with oil into a paste. Of the several different types of Thai curry, green curry paste is the simplest, requiring just a few minutes of assembling and blending.

Making green curry paste: *In a food processor, combine the garlic and chiles and process until minced. Add the basil and process until minced. Add the coriander, salt, pepper, cloves, caraway, and cumin and pulse until evenly blended. With the motor running, slowly pour the oil down the feed tube and process until a paste forms.*

Thai Green Curry Pasta

SERVES 4

Green Curry Paste
4 cloves garlic
2 to 4 serrano chiles, stemmed
¾ cup firmly packed fresh basil, cilantro, or mint leaves
1 teaspoon ground coriander
½ teaspoon salt
½ teaspoon freshly ground black pepper
½ teaspoon ground cloves
½ teaspoon ground caraway
½ teaspoon ground cumin
¼ cup peanut or safflower oil

¾ cup unsweetened coconut milk
¼ cup dry sherry
2 tablespoons Thai or Vietnamese fish sauce
8 ounces dried penne or your favorite pasta
¾ to 1½ pounds cooked meat or seafood (listed on page 78)

Advance Preparation: Prepare the curry paste as shown here. In a bowl, combine the coconut milk, sherry, and fish sauce and mix well. Spoon the curry paste into the coconut milk mixture and stir to combine evenly. (The curry sauce can be covered and refrigerated for up to 8 hours before using.)

Last-Minute Cooking: In a pot, bring 5 quarts of water to a rapid boil over high heat. Lightly salt the water and add the pasta. Cook according to the package instructions for about 12 minutes, until tender. Drain the pasta in a colander and return the empty pot to high heat. Add the sauce and bring to a low boil. Add the meat or seafood and return the pasta to the pot. Stir to combine evenly. Transfer to warmed dinner plates and serve at once.

Menu suggestion: tomato and arugula salad.

Pasta with Olives, Pine Nuts, Lemon, and Chiles

SERVES 4

½ cup pine nuts
4 cloves garlic, minced
3 tablespoons extra virgin olive oil
1 cup heavy cream
¼ cup freshly squeezed lemon juice
½ teaspoon salt
½ teaspoon crushed red pepper flakes
8 ounces dried farfalle, radiatore, or your favorite pasta
¾ to 1½ pounds cooked meat or seafood (listed on page 78)
1 cup pitted imported olives, chopped
1 cup freshly grated imported Parmesan cheese

Advance Preparation: Preheat the oven to 325°F. Spread the pine nuts on a small baking sheet and toast for about 8 minutes, until golden. In a small bowl, combine the garlic and olive oil. In a separate bowl, combine the cream, lemon juice, salt, and pepper flakes and mix well. (All the ingredients except the pine nuts can be covered and refrigerated for up to 8 hours before cooking. Store the pine nuts at room temperature.)

Last-Minute Cooking: In a pot, bring 5 quarts of water to a rapid boil over high heat. Lightly salt the water and add the pasta. Cook according to the package instructions for about 12 minutes, until tender. Drain the pasta in a colander over a bowl and reserve 1 cup of the cooking water. Return the empty pot to high heat. Add the oil mixture and the meat or seafood and cook for about 30 seconds, until the garlic sizzles. Add the olives and the cream mixture and bring to a boil. Return the pasta to the pot and stir to combine evenly. If the pasta appears dry, pour in a small amount of the reserved cooking water and stir until the pasta is lightly glazed with the sauce. Transfer to warmed dinner plates, sprinkle with cheese and pine nuts, and serve at once.

Menu suggestion: chilled asparagus salad.

Italian cooks will often reserve some of the pasta cooking water when draining the pasta. Then, if the pasta seems dry as it is being tossed with its sauce, a little of the reserved pasta water can rescue the dish. Why not just use hot tap water? Because the pasta water has been lightly salted and has taken on the pasta's flavor.

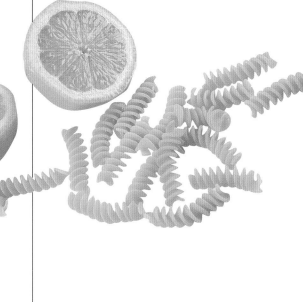

Pasta with Charred Tomatoes

SERVES 4

10 vine-ripe tomatoes
¼ cup sugar
3 tablespoons balsamic vinegar
2 teaspoons Asian chile sauce or your favorite hot sauce
½ teaspoon salt
4 cloves garlic, finely minced
2 tablespoons extra virgin olive oil
8 ounces dried fettuccine, long fusilli, or your favorite pasta
¾ to 1½ pounds cooked meat or seafood (listed on page 78)
¾ cup freshly grated imported Parmesan cheese

Advance Preparation: Prepare a very hot fire in a charcoal grill or preheat a gas grill to high. Char and chop the tomatoes as shown here. You should have about 3 cups. In a bowl, combine the tomatoes, vinegar, chile sauce, and salt and mix well. In a separate bowl, combine the garlic and olive oil. (All the ingredients can be covered and refrigerated for up to 8 hours before using.)

Last-Minute Cooking: In a pot, bring 5 quarts of water to a rapid boil over high heat. Lightly salt the water and add the pasta. Cook according to the package instructions for about 12 minutes, until tender. Drain the pasta in a colander, return the empty pot to high heat, and add the olive oil and garlic. Sauté for about 15 seconds, until the garlic sizzles. Add the tomato mixture and the meat or seafood and bring to a boil. Return the pasta to the pot and stir to combine evenly. Transfer to warmed dinner plates, sprinkle with cheese, and serve at once.

Menu suggestion: crusty bread; cucumber-dill salad.

Charring tomatoes: Cut the top and bottom off each tomato. Cut in half horizontally and sprinkle with the sugar on both sides. When the grill is hot, brush the grill rack with oil and place the tomatoes on the rack. Grill, turning once, for 3 to 4 minutes on each side, until charred. When cool enough to handle, peel and coarsely chop the tomatoes, including seeds.

Pasta with Peanut Butter Glaze

SERVES 4

Peanut Sauce

1/2 cup natural-style peanut butter
2/3 cup chicken broth
1/4 cup red wine vinegar
2 tablespoons thin soy sauce
2 tablespoons dark sesame oil
1 1/2 tablespoons sugar
2 teaspoons Asian chile sauce
1/4 cup chopped cilantro sprigs
2 tablespoons very finely minced ginger

8 ounces dried fusilli or your favorite pasta
3/4 to 1 1/2 pounds cooked meat or seafood (listed on page 78)
4 cups mung bean sprouts
1/3 cup chopped fresh chives

Advance Preparation: To prepare the sauce, in a small bowl, combine all the ingredients and mix well with a whisk. (The sauce can be covered and refrigerated for up to 8 hours before using.)

Last-Minute Cooking: In a pot, bring 5 quarts of lightly salted water to a boil over high heat. Add the pasta and cook according to the package instructions for about 12 minutes, until tender. Drain in a colander over a bowl and reserve 1 cup of the cooking water. Return the empty pot to medium-high heat. Add the meat or seafood and stir for about 1 minute, until warmed. Add the pasta and stir well. Add the bean sprouts and the sauce and stir to combine evenly. If the pasta appears dry, add a small amount of the reserved cooking water and stir until the pasta is lightly glazed with the sauce. Transfer to warmed dinner plates, sprinkle with the chives, and serve at once.

Menu suggestion: iceberg lettuce salad with a dressing from page 106.

Pasta with Blue Cheese

SERVES 4

1 cup chopped walnuts
1/4 cup extra virgin olive oil
5 cloves garlic, finely minced
8 ounces dried penne, fettuccine, or your favorite pasta
3/4 to 1 1/2 pounds cooked meat or seafood (listed on page 78)
5 ounces Gorgonzola or other blue cheese, crumbled
1/4 cup heavy cream
1/2 cup chopped fresh basil
1/2 teaspoon salt
1/4 teaspoon crushed red pepper flakes
Juice of 1 lemon
1 nutmeg, for grating

This recipe is an adaptation of a famous Szechuan peanut or sesame seed paste and noodle dish called Pon Pon Noodles. To make this dish, look for peanut butter whose only ingredients are roasted peanuts and salt. This natural-style peanut butter is much more flavorful than mass-market peanut butters, which are heavily sugared and contain unnecessary additives.

It's hard to stop eating this classic Italian combination of roasted walnuts, Gorgonzola cheese, basil, and pasta. Other blue cheeses that we've enjoyed in this dish are Maytag blue, Stilton, and Danish blue. In this dish, reserving some of the pasta cooking water to add back in at the end of the preparation is essential; it helps melt the blue cheese and create a sauce.

Advance Preparation: Preheat the oven to 325°F. Spread the walnuts on a small baking sheet and toast for about 15 minutes, until darkened. Combine the oil and garlic.

Last-Minute Cooking: In a pot, bring 5 quarts of lightly salted water to a boil over high heat. Add the pasta and cook according to the package instructions for about 12 minutes, until tender. Drain in a colander over a bowl and reserve 1 cup of the cooking water. Return the empty pot to high heat. Add the oil and garlic and sauté for about 15 seconds, until the garlic sizzles. Add the meat or seafood and stir for about 1 minute, until warmed. Return the pasta to the pot and add the cheese, cream, basil, salt, and pepper flakes and stir to combine evenly. Add the reserved cooking water and stir until the cheese starts to melt and a light sauce forms. Sprinkle in the lemon juice and transfer to warmed dinner plates. Grate nutmeg over each serving. Serve at once.

Menu suggestion: mushroom salad with lime-honey dressing (page 106).

Pasta with Coconut-Lemon Curry Sauce

SERVES 4

Coconut-Lemon Curry Sauce
½ cup unsweetened coconut milk
¼ cup chicken broth
¼ cup freshly squeezed lemon juice
2 tablespoons Chinese rice wine or dry sherry
2 tablespoons oyster sauce
1 teaspoon curry powder
1 tablespoon dark sesame oil
1 teaspoon cornstarch
1 teaspoon Asian chile sauce
½ teaspoon sugar
¼ cup chopped cilantro sprigs or fresh basil

3 tablespoons peanut or safflower oil
4 cloves garlic, minced
1 tablespoon finely minced ginger
8 ounces dried fusilli pasta or your favorite pasta
¾ to 1½ pounds cooked meat or seafood (listed on page 78)

For fresh coconut milk, smash a coconut on your driveway. Collect the fragments of the hard white flesh, moving on to the next step when fatigue sets in. Using a vegetable peeler, remove the black skin, bandaging cuts on your hands. Spend no more than 1 hour on this stage. Chop the flesh in a food processor, adding hot water. Transfer the flesh to a clean kitchen towel and twist and squeeze to expel the coconut milk. This is a good forearm exercise. Repeat the process with additional coconuts, or use canned unsweetened coconut milk. No one will know the difference.

Advance Preparation: To prepare the sauce, in a bowl, combine all the ingredients and mix well. In a separate bowl, combine the oil, garlic, and ginger. (The sauce and the oil mixture can be covered and refrigerated for up to 8 hours before cooking.)

Last-Minute Cooking: In a pot, bring 5 quarts of water to a rapid boil over high heat. Lightly salt the water and add the pasta. Cook according to the package instructions for about 12 minutes, until tender. Drain the pasta in a colander and return the empty pot to high heat. Add the oil mixture and sauté for about 15 seconds, until the garlic sizzles. Add the sauce and bring to a boil. Add the meat or seafood and stir well. Return the pasta to the pot and stir to combine evenly. Transfer to warmed dinner plates and serve at once.

Menu suggestion: salad greens and sliced apples with a dressing from page 106.

Wraps: Tacos, Mu Shu, and More

Spicy Wok Wraps

SERVES 2 TO 3

1 pound ground beef or lamb
3 cloves garlic, minced
3 tablespoons hoisin sauce
2 tablespoons oyster sauce
1 tablespoon dark sesame oil
1 tablespoon Asian chile sauce
¼ cup chicken broth
1 teaspoon cornstarch
1 mango or papaya
8 (6-inch) flour tortillas or pita breads
2 tablespoons peanut or safflower oil
1 cup cilantro sprigs

Advance Preparation: Place the meat in a bowl and add the garlic, hoisin sauce, oyster sauce, sesame oil, and chile sauce. Using your hands, mix thoroughly. In a separate bowl, combine the broth and cornstarch and mix well. Peel the mango and cut into thin strips. (All the ingredients can be covered and refrigerated for up to 8 hours before using.)

Last-Minute Cooking: To warm the tortillas, preheat the oven to 325°F. Stack the tortillas and wrap in aluminum foil. Place the tortillas in the oven and heat for 15 minutes. Place a wok over high heat. When the wok is hot, add the peanut oil and roll around the sides of the wok. When the oil is hot, add the meat mixture. Cook, pressing the meat against the sides of the pan, for about 2 minutes, until it breaks into individual clumps and loses its pink color. Stir the broth mixture and add to the wok. Cook, stirring, for 30 seconds. Transfer the meat to warmed dinner plates. To assemble, place some mango, cilantro, and meat in each tortilla, roll into a cylinder, and eat out of hand.

Menu suggestion: watercress and bean sprout salad.

Seared Wok Chicken with Charred Tortillas

SERVES 2 TO 3

8 (6-inch) flour tortillas
2 tablespoons white sesame seeds
1 pound boneless, skinless chicken breast or thigh meat
2 green onions, white and green parts, chopped
¼ cup chopped cilantro sprigs
2 tablespoons finely minced ginger
3 tablespoons hoisin sauce
2 tablespoons dark sesame oil
2 tablespoons dry sherry
2 tablespoons thin soy sauce
1 tablespoon Asian chile sauce (optional)
2 tablespoons peanut or safflower oil
4 cups shredded iceberg lettuce
½ cup store-bought or homemade salsa

Advance Preparation: Lightly char the tortillas on both sides over a medium-heat barbecue or a gas burner. Stack the tortillas and wrap in aluminum foil. Place the sesame seeds in a dry sauté pan over medium heat and toast for about 2 minutes, until golden. Cut the chicken into ½-inch cubes or very thin rectangles. Place the chicken in a bowl and add the sesame seeds, onions, cilantro, ginger, hoisin sauce, sesame oil, sherry, soy sauce, and chile sauce and mix well. Cover and refrigerate the chicken for at least 10 minutes and up to 8 hours. Store the tortillas at room temperature until ready to use.

Last-Minute Cooking: To reheat the tortillas, preheat the oven to 325°F. Place the tortillas, still wrapped in foil, in the oven and heat for 15 minutes. Place a wok over high heat. When the wok is hot, add the peanut oil and roll around the sides of the wok. When the oil is hot, add the chicken. Stir and toss for about 2 minutes, until it loses its pink color. Transfer to warmed dinner plates. Serve at once, accompanied by the lettuce, salsa, and tortillas.

Menu suggestion: avocado salad with a dressing from page 106.

Corn and flour tortillas made in Mexico are marvels of tenderness and flavor—you can often find them in Latin markets. Unfortunately, the tortillas sold in supermarkets don't quite measure up. We've found that the best way to rejuvenate supermarket tortillas is to lightly char them over a gas burner or on a grill for about 5 seconds on each side. Stacked and wrapped in aluminum foil, they'll still be perfectly tender even if rewarmed hours later.

Barbecued Fish Tacos with Pineapple Salsa

SERVES 4

4 (6-ounce) fresh firm fish fillets, such as sea bass, halibut, or mahimahi
1/3 cup white wine
3 tablespoons thin soy sauce
1/2 teaspoon freshly ground black pepper
12 crisp taco shells
2 limes, cut into wedges

Salsa

1/2 fresh pineapple, peeled and cored
2 tablespoons minced green onions
1/4 cup minced cilantro sprigs or fresh basil
2 tablespoons freshly squeezed orange juice
2 tablespoons brown sugar
2 tablespoons Thai or Vietnamese fish sauce or thin soy sauce
1 teaspoon Asian chile sauce

Advance Preparation: Place the fish in a shallow, nonreactive container. Combine the wine, soy sauce, and pepper and mix well. To prepare the salsa, coarsely chop the pineapple. You should have about 2 cups. Place the pineapple in a bowl and add the green onions, cilantro, orange juice, brown sugar, fish sauce, and chile sauce and stir well. (All the ingredients can be covered and refrigerated for up to 8 hours before using.)

Last-Minute Cooking: Prepare a medium fire in a charcoal grill or preheat a gas grill to medium. Pour the wine mixture over the fish and marinate for 5 to 15 minutes. When the grill is hot, brush the grill rack with oil and place the fish on the rack. Grill, turning once, for 3 to 4 minutes on each side, until the flesh flakes with slight pressure from a fork. Transfer the fish to warmed dinner plates. Serve at once, accompanied by the salsa, taco shells, and lime wedges.

Menu suggestion: steamed corn with herb butter.

Fish tacos are popular everywhere along the Mexican coast. Though in Mexico, tacos are made with soft corn or flour tortillas, here we've substituted crisp taco shells common in Mexican-American cooking. Simple to make, with intense flavor, tacos come in many variations. Replace our marinade with your favorite fish barbecue sauce, or use any oil and vinegar salad dressing. For the pineapple, you can substitute 2 cups chopped ripe mango or papaya, thinly sliced firm banana, or chopped tomatoes. If you substitute tomatoes, use juicy vine-ripe ones from your garden or a summertime farmers' market.

Separating lettuce leaves: *Slice the bottom off the lettuce head and then gently peel off individual leaves to use as cups. Trim large leaves into smaller cups using poultry shears or scissors.*

Wok-Blasted Pork in Lettuce Cups

SERVES 2 TO 4

Wok-Blast Marinade
2 tablespoons hoisin sauce
2 tablespoons dry sherry
1 tablespoon dark soy sauce
1 tablespoon oyster sauce
1 tablespoon dark sesame oil
1 tablespoon Asian chile sauce
3 cloves garlic, finely minced
2 green onions, white and green parts, chopped

1 pound fresh pork tenderloin, silver skin removed (page 56)
1/3 cup pine nuts
1 head iceberg lettuce
2 tablespoons peanut or safflower oil
1/2 cup hoisin sauce

Advance Preparation: To prepare the marinade, in a large bowl, combine all the ingredients and mix well. Cut the pork into matchstick pieces, add to the marinade, and stir to coat evenly. Cover and refrigerate for at least 10 minutes and up to 8 hours. Preheat the oven to 325°F. Spread the pine nuts on a small baking sheet and toast for about 8 minutes, until golden. Gently separate the lettuce leaves to use as cups. Cut larger leaves in half. (The lettuce can be covered and refrigerated up to 8 hours before using.)

Last-Minute Cooking: Place a wok over high heat. When the wok is hot, add the peanut oil and roll around the sides of the wok. When the oil is hot, add the pork. Stir and toss for 2 to 3 minutes, until it loses its pink color. Stir in the pine nuts. Transfer to warmed dinner plates. Serve at once, accompanied by the lettuce cups and hoisin sauce. To assemble, place a small amount of hoisin sauce in each lettuce cup, add some pork, and eat out of hand.

Menu suggestion: jicama salad with a dressing from page 106.

Vietnamese Shrimp Salad with Rice Paper

Of the many different wrappings used in Vietnamese cuisine, rice paper is the most common. The paper is made by drying circles of rice paste on bamboo mats, which gives the dried sheets an attractive basket-weave texture. Sold in every Asian market, the sheets need to be softened in warm water. Moistened too much, the rice paper disintegrates; moistened too little, the paper breaks upon the first bend. If rice paper is not available, warmed tortillas can be substituted. Although this recipe provides directions for a Vietnamese salad dressing, we have often used an oil and vinegar herb dressing with equally satisfying results.

Softening rice paper: *Handling the rice paper gently, immerse in very hot water for 5 seconds, then lay on a flat surface. After 30 seconds, use hot water to moisten any parts that have not become pliable.*

SERVES 4

6 cups baby salad greens
1 cup loosely packed cilantro sprigs
2 tablespoons freshly squeezed lime juice
2 tablespoons light brown sugar
2 tablespoons Thai or Vietnamese fish sauce
2 tablespoons peanut or safflower oil
2 teaspoons Asian chile sauce
2 cloves garlic, minced
1 tablespoon finely minced ginger
2 ripe mangos
1½ pounds cooked shelled shrimp, chilled
1 cup unsalted roasted peanuts
8 (8-inch) sheets Vietnamese rice paper
Peanut sauce (page 86) or spicy salsa (optional)

Advance Preparation: In a large bowl, combine the greens and cilantro and toss well. In a separate bowl, combine the lime juice, sugar, fish sauce, oil, chile sauce, garlic, and ginger and mix well. Peel the mangos and cut into bite-sized pieces. (All the ingredients can be covered and refrigerated for up to 8 hours before using.)

Last-Minute Cooking: In a bowl, combine the greens, mangos, shrimp, and peanuts and toss well. Stir the dressing, add to the greens, and toss to coat evenly. Soften a rice paper sheet as shown here. Spoon one-eighth of the salad mixture onto the softened sheet and roll into a cylinder. Repeat with remaining rice paper sheets and filling. Transfer to dinner plates and serve at once, accompanied by peanut sauce.

Menu suggestion: deli-bought couscous salad.

Mu Shu Vegetables

SERVES 2 TO 4

8 (8-inch) flour tortillas
4 eggs
2 tablespoons dark sesame oil
¼ head green cabbage
¼ pound fresh button mushrooms, caps tightly closed
3 green onions, white and green parts
3 cloves garlic, finely minced
2 tablespoons oyster sauce
2 tablespoons Chinese rice wine or dry sherry
1 teaspoon Asian chile sauce
1 teaspoon cornstarch
3 tablespoons peanut or safflower oil
½ cup hoisin sauce

Advance Preparation: Lightly char the tortillas on both sides over a medium-heat barbecue or a gas burner. Stack the tortillas and wrap in aluminum foil. In a small bowl, beat the eggs until well blended. Stir in 1 tablespoon of the sesame oil. Shred the cabbage. Cut the mushrooms through the stems into ⅛-inch slices. Chop the green onions. In a bowl, combine the cabbage, mushrooms, green onions, and garlic and mix well. In a small bowl, combine the oyster sauce, rice wine, chile sauce, cornstarch, and remaining 1 tablespoon sesame oil and mix well. (All the ingredients except the tortillas can be covered and refrigerated for up to 8 hours before cooking. Store the tortillas at room temperature.)

Last-Minute Cooking: To reheat the tortillas, preheat the oven to 325°F. Place the tortillas, still wrapped in foil, in the oven and heat for 15 minutes. Place a wok over high heat. When the wok is hot, add 1½ tablespoons of the peanut oil. When the oil is hot, add the eggs. Scramble the eggs for about 2 minutes, until firmly set, then transfer to a plate. Return the wok to high heat and add the remaining 1½ tablespoons peanut oil. When the oil is hot, add the vegetable mixture. Stir-fry for about 1 minute, until the color brightens. Add the oyster sauce mixture and stir well. Return the eggs to the wok and mix briefly. Transfer to warmed dinner plates. Serve at once, accompanied by the hoisin sauce and tortillas. To assemble, spread a small amount of hoisin sauce on a tortilla, add some vegetables, roll the tortilla into a cylinder, and eat.

Menu suggestion: Chinese restaurant hot and sour soup.

Mu shu is one of the most famous stir-fry dishes from northern China. The name derives from a yellow blossom that appears in Beijing in the spring, represented in all mu shu preparations by scrambled eggs.

Rolling mu shu: *Spread hoisin sauce on the tortillas. Add a row of the stir-fry filling down the center of the tortilla. Roll into a cylinder and fold one end over.*

Spicy Beef Chili in Pita Bread

SERVES 4

1 cup red wine
½ cup ketchup
2 tablespoons Heinz 57 sauce
2 tablespoons chili powder
2 tablespoons brown sugar
2 tablespoons chopped fresh oregano leaves, basil leaves, or cilantro sprigs
1 tablespoon your favorite hot sauce
½ teaspoon salt
2 tablespoons olive oil
1 yellow onion, chopped
1½ pounds ground beef, lamb, pork, or meatloaf mix
6 cloves garlic, minced
8 pita breads
1 cup shredded sharp cheddar cheese
¼ head iceberg lettuce, shredded

Advance Preparation: In a bowl, combine the wine, ketchup, 57 sauce, chili powder, sugar, oregano, hot sauce, and salt and mix well. Place a heavy sauté pan over medium heat. When the pan is hot, add the oil and onion. Cook for about 6 minutes, until the onion browns. Add the meat and garlic and cook, pressing the meat against the sides of the pan, for about 4 minutes, until it separates into individual clumps and loses its pink color. Add the wine mixture and bring to boil. Decrease the heat to achieve a simmer and cook for about 10 minutes, until nearly all the liquid cooks away. Stack the pita breads and wrap in aluminum foil. (All the ingredients can be covered and refrigerated for up to 8 hours.)

Last-Minute Cooking: Preheat the oven to 325°F. Place the pita breads, still wrapped in foil, in the oven and heat for 15 minutes. Reheat the chili over medium heat, tasting and adjusting the seasoning with salt if necessary. Transfer the chili to warmed soup bowls. To assemble, spoon some chili into a pita bread, add some cheese and lettuce, and eat out of hand.

Menu suggestions: corn bread muffins; salad greens with oil and vinegar dressing.

Pita bread makes an ideal vessel for stir-fries, homemade chili, and stews. While all the recipes in this book call for wrapping pita bread in aluminum foil to warm in the oven, you can add a more complex taste by using the charring technique described for tortillas on page 89.

Tropical Shrimp Tacos

This recipe lends itself to endless variations. Toasted pecans, peanuts, almonds, and pine nuts can all be substituted for the walnuts. Mangos, papayas, peaches, and nectarines can be used in place of the bananas. If you don't want to mince the chiles, whose oil can irritate the skin, use 1 to 2 teaspoons of your favorite hot sauce instead. Lastly, while the recipe indicates cilantro or mint, other herbs that work well here are basil, flat-leaf Italian parsley, and oregano.

SERVES 3 TO 4

¾ cup chopped walnuts
1 pound large shrimp, shelled and deveined
3 cloves garlic, finely minced
1 to 3 fresh serrano chiles, minced including seeds
2 tablespoons freshly squeezed lime juice
2 tablespoons brown sugar
2 tablespoons Thai or Vietnamese fish sauce
¼ cup chopped cilantro sprigs or fresh mint
1 ripe avocado
2 firm bananas
8 (8-inch) flour tortillas or crisp taco shells
2 tablespoons peanut or safflower oil

Advance Preparation: Preheat the oven to 325°F. Spread the walnuts on a small baking sheet and toast for about 15 minutes, until darkened. Split the shrimp in half lengthwise. In a small bowl, combine the garlic, chiles, lime juice, sugar, fish sauce, and cilantro and mix well. Seed, peel, and thinly slice the avocado. Peel the bananas, cut in half lengthwise, and cut into small cubes. Stir the avocado and banana into the lime juice mixture. Stack the tortillas and wrap in aluminum foil. Do not stack the taco shells. (All the ingredients except the walnuts and tortillas can be covered and refrigerated for up to 8 hours before using. Store the walnuts and tortillas at room temperature.)

Last-Minute Cooking: Preheat the oven to 325°F. Place the tortillas, still wrapped in foil, in the oven and heat for 15 minutes. Place a large sauté pan over high heat. When very hot, add the oil. When the oil is hot, add the shrimp and sauté for about 1 minute, until pink. Add the walnuts and sauté for about 1 minute, until the shrimp are fully cooked. Transfer to warmed dinner plates. Serve at once, accompanied by the avocado and banana salsa and the tortillas.

Menu suggestion: deli-bought gazpacho.

Chicken-Shiitake Tacos

SERVES 3 TO 4

1 cup pecans
1 deli-bought roast chicken
½ pound fresh shiitake mushrooms
½ cup heavy cream
¼ cup white wine or chicken broth
2 tablespoons oyster sauce
1 teaspoon Asian chile sauce or your favorite hot sauce
½ teaspoon grated orange zest
8 (8-inch) flour tortillas or crisp taco shells
2 tablespoons peanut or safflower oil
1 tablespoon unsalted butter
¼ cup chopped fresh parsley leaves or cilantro sprigs

Advance Preparation: Preheat the oven to 325°F. Spread the pecans on a small baking sheet and toast for about 15 minutes, until darkened. Pull the chicken meat off the bones, discard the skin, and cut the meat into matchstick pieces. You should have 3 to 4 cups. Cut off and discard the mushroom stems and cut the caps into ¼-inch slices. In a bowl, combine the cream, wine, oyster sauce, chile sauce, and orange zest and mix well. Stack the tortillas and wrap in aluminum foil. Do not stack the taco shells. (All the ingredients except the pecans and tortillas can be covered and refrigerated for up to 8 hours before using. Store the pecans and tortillas at room temperature.)

Last-Minute Cooking: Preheat the oven to 325°F. Place the tortillas, still wrapped in foil, in the oven and heat for 15 minutes. Place a large sauté pan over high heat. When the pan is hot, add the oil and butter. When the butter melts, add the mushrooms and sauté for 2 minutes, until the mushrooms begin to shrink in size. Add the chicken and the cream mixture. Cook for 3 to 5 minutes, until the mushrooms wilt and the sauce glazes the food. Stir in the nuts and parsley. Transfer to warmed dinner plates and serve at once, accompanied by the tortillas.

Menu suggestion: Caesar salad with crumbled bacon and chile croutons.

Fresh shiitakes should feel dense, firm, and dry when purchased. If light-weighted, they have become dehydrated during long storage and will suffer a lack of flavor. If wet, they have been incorrectly stored in a sealed container and will have a mushy texture. Shiitake stems are always tough and should be pared off and discarded or used in making stock. As for washing shiitakes, it's not only unnecessary, it's detrimental. The mushrooms are grown on compressed wood in cement-floored, climate-controlled sheds and never come in contact with compost or dirt. If you wash shiitakes, they quickly acquire an unpleasant soft texture.

Side Dishes for Fast Entrées

Breads, Pastas, and Grains Ready from the Market

Fresh: breads, dinner rolls, flour and whole wheat tortillas, pita bread, pasta, ravioli, and tortellini.

Frozen: bread, garlic bread, dinner rolls, ravioli, tortellini, potato pancakes, home fries, and twice-baked potatoes.

Prepackaged: rice pilaf, couscous, quinoa, long-grain and wild rice mix, brown and wild rice mix, basmati and wild rice mix, pecan wild rice, curry rice pilaf, New Orleans–style yellow rice, pearled wheat and bulgur mix, and stovetop corn bread mix.

Deli: potato, rice, and pasta dishes.

Vegetables Ready from the Market

Fresh: precut broccoli, baby carrots, coleslaw mixes, prepared stir-fry mixes (to steam, blanch, microwave, sauté, or stir-fry).

Frozen: avoid.

Canned: avoid.

Salads Ready from the Market

Fresh: green salad mixes, freshly cut fruit, toasted nuts, and croutons.

Prepackaged: refrigerated salad dressings.

Deli: prepared salads.

BREAD, PASTA, AND GRAIN SIDE DISHES

Chinese-Style Steamed Rice

SERVES 4

1 cup long-grain white rice
½ teaspoon salt

Preparation and Cooking: Place the rice in a fine-mesh sieve and rinse under cold running water for about 2 minutes, until the water runs clear. Transfer the rice to a saucepan. Add enough cold water to cover by 1 inch. Add the salt and place over medium-high heat and bring to a vigorous boil. When the water just begins to evaporate and the rice has small craters across the surface, cover the saucepan and decrease the heat to achieve a simmer. Cook for 15 minutes, never lifting the lid, until all the water has evaporated and the rice is tender. Serve within 20 minutes.

Never use instant or converted rice, neither of which tastes as good as California or Texas long-grain white rice, Thai jasmine rice, or Indian basmati rice. One cup of raw rice will expand to 4 cups cooked.

Rice Pilaf

SERVES 6

1½ cups long-grain white rice
2 tablespoons olive, peanut, or safflower oil
½ cup dried currants (optional)
3 cups chicken broth
½ to 1 teaspoon salt
½ cup chopped fresh parsley (optional)

Preparation and Cooking: Place the rice in a fine-mesh sieve and rinse under cold running water until the water runs clear. Place a saucepan over medium-high heat. When the pan is hot, heat the oil. Add the rice and sauté, stirring, for 1 minute, until coated with the oil. Add the currants and broth and salt to taste and stir well. Cook, stirring occasionally, until the liquid comes to a low boil. Cover and decrease the heat to achieve a simmer. Cook for 18 minutes, never lifting the lid, until all the water has evaporated and the rice is tender. Stir in the parsley and serve at once.

This rice pilaf can be made up to a day in advance, and then reheated in the microwave. To reheat, transfer the rice to a microwave-safe bowl, cover with plastic wrap, and microwave on high until piping hot.

Oven-Roasted New Potatoes

SERVES 4

6 cups small new potatoes, about 3 pounds
Extra virgin olive oil
Salt
Freshly ground black pepper
1 to 4 cloves garlic, finely minced (optional)
½ cup chopped fresh parsley (optional)

Preparation and Cooking: Preheat the oven to 400°F. Leave the potatoes whole or, to quicken cooking, cut in half. Place the potatoes in a bowl. Toss with enough oil to very lightly coat the surfaces. Add the salt, pepper, and garlic to taste, and toss to combine evenly. Transfer to a shallow baking pan and place in the oven. Bake for about 30 minutes, until easily pierced with a fork. Sprinkle with parsley and serve within 10 minutes. (The potatoes can also be kept hot in a 225°F oven for 30 minutes before serving.)

This is an extremely easy and delicious side dish. As an alternate to roasting, the potatoes can also be browned in a sauté pan on the stovetop, then covered and cooked over low heat.

Mashed Potatoes

SERVES 4

4 russet potatoes, about 1½ pounds, peeled and cut into quarters
½ cup milk, at room temperature
4 tablespoons butter or sour cream, at room temperature
1 teaspoon salt
Freshly ground black pepper

Preparation and Cooking: Place the potatoes in a saucepan and add cold water to cover. Place the saucepan over medium-high heat and bring to a boil. Decrease the heat to achieve a simmer and cook for 20 to 25 minutes, until easily pierced with a fork. Alternatively, place the potatoes in a microwave-safe dish, cover with plastic wrap, and cook on high for 5 to 8 minutes, stirring every 4 minutes. Drain the potatoes and return to the saucepan or microwave dish. Mash the potatoes with a fork or potato masher or pass through a food mill or ricer. Add the milk, butter, and salt and pepper to taste and continue mashing until desired consistency is achieved. Serve at once.

Mashed potatoes can be made ahead and kept warm for up to 3 hours in a metal bowl, covered with plastic wrap, set over a saucepan of barely simmering water.

Pasta—Three Variations

SERVES 4

8 ounces your favorite shape dried pasta
Salt
Freshly ground black pepper
¼ cup freshly grated imported Parmesan cheese

Preparation and Cooking: In a saucepan, bring 4 to 5 quarts of water to a boil over medium-high heat. Lightly salt the water and add the pasta. Cook for about 12 minutes, until tender. Drain the pasta in a colander over a bowl and reserve 1 cup of the cooking water. Return the empty pot to medium heat.

For Pesto Pasta:
Return the cooked pasta to the pot, add ½ cup store-bought pesto sauce, and stir well until evenly combined. If the sauce seems too dry, stir in some of the reserved cooking water. Season with salt and pepper to taste, sprinkle with cheese, and serve at once.

For Tomato Sauce Pasta:
Add 1 cup store-bought tomato pasta sauce to the pot and bring to a boil. Return the cooked pasta to the pot and stir well until evenly combined. If the pasta seems too dry, stir in some of the reserved cooking water. Season with salt and pepper to taste, sprinkle with cheese, and serve at once.

For Olive Oil Pasta:
Return the cooked pasta to the pot, add ¼ cup olive oil and ¼ cup chopped fresh parsley, and stir well until evenly combined. If the pasta seems too dry, stir in some of the reserved cooking water. Season with salt and pepper to taste, sprinkle with cheese, and serve at once.

Garlic Bread

SERVES 4

1 loaf sweet- or sourdough bread
½ cup unsalted butter, at room temperature
4 cloves garlic, finely minced
Salt
Freshly ground black pepper
¼ cup freshly grated imported Parmesan cheese

Preparation and Cooking: Preheat the broiler. Place a rack 4 inches from the heating element. Using a serrated knife, cut the bread in half horizontally. Spread with the butter and sprinkle on the garlic, salt and pepper to taste, and cheese. Cut crosswise partway through the bread to form equal-sized serving pieces. Place the bread on a baking sheet and broil for 4 to 5 minutes, until golden. Serve at once.

VEGETABLE SIDE DISHES

*W*hat's the point of making a fast entrée if the side dishes take an arduous amount of time? Prepare just one vegetable with one of the cooking techniques outlined on the following pages, pair with simple seasonings, and you've got a great accompaniment. Steamed asparagus drizzled with a little balsamic vinegar, sautéed zucchini with butter, salt, and pepper, and blanched carrots tossed with soy sauce and black pepper are all examples of tasty and fast side dishes.

Seasoning Elements: Use one or a combination of the following seasonings to flavor steamed, blanched, microwaved, sautéed, or stir-fried vegetables. Directions for each of these cooking methods can be found on the following pages.

1 to 3 tablespoons unsalted butter, at room temperature
1 to 3 tablespoons extra virgin olive oil
1 to 3 tablespoons thin soy sauce
1 to 3 tablespoons balsamic vinegar
1 to 3 tablespoons homemade or store-bought oil and vinegar salad dressing
Salt
Freshly ground black pepper

Steaming Vegetables

*S*teaming is a quick and nutritious way to prepare vegetables. The key tool is a stainless steel collapsible steamer designed to fit into saucepans. You can also use a metal or bamboo Chinese steamer that fits over a wok, found in all Asian markets.

Choose one of the following vegetables: asparagus, broccoli, Brussels sprouts, carrots, cauliflower, Chinese long beans, corn, green beans, snow peas, or summer squash (crookneck, pattypan, zucchini). Pour water into a saucepan to a depth of 1½ inches and bring to a furious boil over high heat. Leave the vegetables whole or cut into bite-sized pieces. Place in the steamer tray(s), allowing enough room for the steam to circulate through the vegetables. Place the steamer in the saucepan and cover. The vegetables are perfectly cooked when they become brightly colored and are tender. Transfer the vegetables to a serving dish and sprinkle with one or more of the seasonings listed above. Toss to combine evenly and serve at once.

Blanching Vegetables

*T*he key to blanching is to cook the vegetables only until they brighten in color and are crisp-tender, and then drain immediately in a colander. Once the bright color leaches from the vegetables, they are transformed to a mushy mess.

Choose one of the following firm vegetables: asparagus, broccoli, Brussels sprouts, baby carrots, cauliflower, Chinese long beans, corn, or green beans. Bring a saucepan full of water to a rapid boil over high heat. Leave asparagus, baby carrots, and green beans whole; separate broccoli and cauliflower into individual flowerets; and halve Brussels sprouts. Add the vegetables to the boiling water and stir. Since the cooking process is very quick, stir often. Thick asparagus will be done in about 1 minute; long beans and corn in 2 minutes; broccoli, baby carrots, and cauliflower in about

*W*hen steaming, to avoid scalding yourself be very careful when removing the lid of the pan.

3 minutes; green beans in 6 to 10 minutes; and Brussels sprouts in 10 minutes. The moment the vegetables become brightly colored and are tender, drain in a colander. Transfer the vegetables to a serving dish and sprinkle with one or more of the seasonings listed on page 104. Toss to combine evenly and serve at once.

Microwaving Vegetables

Microwaving is a wonderful method for quickly cooking vegetables, whether whole or cut into pieces. Corn and artichokes cook in minutes and wilted spinach is accomplished without a messy sauté pan.

Choose one of the following vegetables: asparagus, broccoli flowerets, Brussels sprouts, carrots (1-inch pieces), cauliflower flowerets, Chinese long beans, corn, green beans, snow peas, or summer squash (crookneck, pattypan, or zucchini in 1-inch pieces). Place the vegetables on a microwave-safe plate and cover with plastic wrap. Microwave on high, stirring every 3 minutes, until tender. Transfer the vegetables to a serving dish and sprinkle with one or more of the seasonings listed on page 104. Toss to combine evenly and serve at once.

Sautéing Vegetables

Because sautéing requires your constant attention, you should only choose this technique if your fast entrée is being barbecued or roasted—not sautéed, boiled, or broiled.

Choose one of the following vegetables to serve 4 people: up to 6 cups bite-size pieces of asparagus, bell peppers, broccoli, Brussels sprouts, carrots, cauliflower, Chinese long beans, corn, green beans, firm mushrooms, snow peas, or summer squash (crookneck, pattypan, zucchini); or up to 8 cups of coarsely chopped cabbage, kale, and spinach. Place a large sauté pan over medium-high heat. When the pan is hot, add 1 to 3 tablespoons butter or peanut, safflower, corn, or olive oil. When the butter is hot, add the vegetables and sauté until leafy vegetables have just wilted and other vegetables are tender. If the vegetables appear about to scorch but are not yet tender, add about ¼ cup of water, chicken broth, or white wine. The added moisture will create steam and speed the cooking. Transfer the vegetables to a serving dish and sprinkle with one or more of the seasonings listed on page 104. Toss to combine evenly and serve at once.

Stir-Frying Vegetables

As with sautéing, choose the stir-frying method only when your main dish does not requires your constant attention during cooking.

Choose one of the following vegetables to serve 2 to 3 people: asparagus, bell peppers, bok choy, cabbage, celery, firm mushrooms, onions, snow peas, or summer squash (crookneck, pattypan, zucchini). Cut into bite-sized pieces. You should have no more than 4 cups. Place a wok over high heat. When the wok is very hot, add 2 tablespoons peanut or safflower oil. Roll the oil around the sides of the wok. When the oil just begins to smoke, add the vegetables. Stir and toss until the vegetables become brightly colored and are tender. If the vegetables seem about to scorch but are not yet tender, add about 2 tablespoons of water, chicken broth, or white wine. When tender, transfer the vegetables to a serving dish and sprinkle with one or more of the seasonings listed on page 104, or with your favorite wok sauce. Toss to combine evenly and serve at once.

When microwaving vegetables, always stir them every 3 minutes to achieve even cooking.

For a flavorful and easy Asian vegetable stir-fry sauce, combine 2 tablespoons oyster sauce, 1 tablespoon dark sesame oil, ½ teaspoon sugar, and ⅛ teaspoon freshly ground black pepper and mix well. Add the sauce to the wok during the final seconds of stir-frying.

QUICK SALADS

Repeating what we advised at the beginning of the book, when pinched for time, serve either a salad or a vegetable dish, *but never both*. No one is going to miss one or the other, and you won't be forced into culinary servitude!

For a dinner salad, you need approximately 1 cup (1 handful) of greens per person. This can be one lettuce or any combination of lettuces or prepackaged salad mixes. All you need to add for a satisfying salad to accompany your fast entrée is 1 sliced ripe avocado or papaya; a little grated Parmesan or crumbled blue or goat cheese; and a scattering of toasted nuts. Toss the salad with a store-bought dressing (see sidebar) or try one of the homemade dressings found below.

Lime-Honey Dressing

¼ cup freshly squeezed lime or lemon juice
3 tablespoons extra virgin olive oil
3 tablespoons honey
½ teaspoon ground cumin
½ teaspoon salt
½ teaspoon freshly ground black pepper or your favorite hot sauce
1 small clove garlic, finely minced
2 tablespoons chopped cilantro sprigs, mint leaves, or basil leaves

Combine all of the ingredients in a jar, cover with the lid, and shake thoroughly. If made in advance, the dressing can be stored in the refrigerator for no more than 2 days. Makes enough to dress 6 cups of salad.

Blue Cheese Dressing

¼ cup crumbled blue cheese
6 tablespoons extra virgin olive oil
3 tablespoons balsamic vinegar
2 tablespoons thin soy sauce
¼ teaspoon freshly ground black pepper

Combine all of the ingredients in a jar, cover with the lid, and shake thoroughly. If made in advance, the dressing can be stored in the refrigerator for no more than 4 days. Makes enough to dress 6 cups of salad.

Ginger-Citrus Dressing

2 tablespoons finely minced ginger
¼ cup chopped fresh basil leaves, mint leaves, or cilantro sprigs
1 teaspoon grated orange zest
⅓ cup peanut or safflower oil
¼ cup freshly squeezed orange juice
¼ cup balsamic vinegar
½ teaspoon Asian chile sauce or your favorite hot sauce

Combine all of the ingredients in a jar, cover with the lid, and shake thoroughly. If made in advance, the dressing can be stored in the refrigerator for no more than 2 days. Makes enough to dress 8 cups of salad.

Acknowledgments

Many friends helped bring this book into print and we are deeply appreciative of your support and many contributions. Thank you Ten Speed Press, particularly Phil Wood; our publisher, Kirsty Melville; and Jo Ann Deck and Dennis Hayes in special sales. Many thanks also to our editor Holly Taines White, who did a wonderful job molding the book into its final form. Our friend and book designer, Beverly Wilson, Napa Valley, California, contributed her unique vision and added so much to our pleasure working on this book. Julie Smith, San Anselmo, California, was the food stylist, and added her culinary and artistic skills to the photography. And Steve Ruggenberg helped Hugh test many of the recipes. It was wonderful to work with all of you on this exciting book!

After the recipes were tested at our home and used in cooking classes, the following home cooks gave a final evaluation. This book gained much from their insights. Thank you Carol Bassett, Kathleen Bergin, Brad and Vicki Billington, Jo Bowen, Linda Butler, Geri Campbell, Bill and Lynda Casper, Pamela and Mike Cincola, Cheryl Connolly, Shari Conrad, Kris Cox, Debra Crow, Debbie Crowther, Lucy Cundiff, Steve and Joy Davey, Kim and George David, Judy Bonzi Dubrawski, Sue Evanicky, Gaven Fahl, Ray Finfer, Suzanne Figi, Diane and Colin Forkner, Suzy Fostter, Janie and Ron Frazar, Marilynn Gantz, Sharie and Ron Goldfarb, Tracie Goudlock, Jennifer and Mike Graley, Maureen and Jerry Guon, Michele Hamilton, Kathryn Haslach, Margaret Healey, Joann Hecht, Judy Hoovler, Mary Catherine Huff, Linda and Ron Johnson, Bruce and Lynn Kaplan, Candy and Gil Katen, Gail and Chuck Kendall, Lou and Bettlu Kessler, Yun Kim, Walter Kinney and Kathy Mason, Sydene Kober, Terry and Irene Koch, Jeannie Komsky, Bobbie and Paul Kouri, Susan Krueger, Diana and Richard Langston, Kim and Amee Lockhart, Paula Maguire, Shelly Massey, Jennifer McIntosh, Richard Mitchell, Cheryl Parker, George and Estee Plavec, Diana Pleva, Colleen Ploch, Barbara and Tom Pridham, Lynn and James Prude, Judy Radcliffe-Heyman, Jill Rogge, Paul Salzinger, Ian Scott, Ryan Sinkus, Valerie Sinkus, Christine Stalder, Ken and Diane Thompson, Bob and Judy Torries, Glenna Valley, Victoria Wells, Jennifer Yonstra, Karen Young, and Carol Zwicker.

Artist Credits

We are so happy to have had many old and new friends provide their beautiful tabletop wares for the photography in this cookbook. The endlessly creative Julie Sanders of the Cyclamen Collection in Oakland, California, provided a vast rainbow of ceramic dishes for the photos on pages 21, 24, 32, 40, 46, 51, 62, 73, 76, 90, and 93. Thank you Julie! Ceramic artist Kathy Erteman of New York City made the graphic black and white pieces on the cover and on pages 1 and 102.

Many thanks also to the St. Helena Olive Oil Company in Rutherford, California, for the dishes and accessories on pages 29 and 43. The Raku Gallery in Yountville, California, provided the Steven McGovney and Tammy Camarot ceramic plate on page 96, as well as the All-U-Can-Handle flatware on pages 43, 46, and 96. The Oakville Grocery in Oakville, California, was the source for the lovely dishes on page 81.

We show the Benecia, California, master glassblower Michael Nourot's new work in the bowls on pages 37 and 107. Thanks also to glass artist Stephen Smyers of Benecia, California, who made the glass stemware shown on pages 37 and 46, and to John Cook of Oregon for the glass on page 29.

Vanderbilt's Gallery in St. Helena, California, provided the glasses on pages 51 and 93; the flatware, napkin, and glasses on pages 65 and 76; and the Aletha Soule ceramic ware on page 84. The Thia Gallery in Berkeley, California, was the source for the beautiful Scott O'Dell footed dish and the Iro hand-painted textile on page 54, and the O'Dell glassware on page 68. The Culinary Institute of America at Greystone in St. Helena, California, provided the Guy Buffet clock from Santa Barbara Ceramic Design on page 109, as well as the equipment and tools shown on pages 14 and 15.

Thank you all for being part of *Fast Entrées*!

Conversion Charts

Liquid Measurements

Cups and Spoons	Fluid Ounces	Approximate Metric Term	Approximate Centiliters	Actual Milliliters
1 tsp	⅙ oz	*	½ cL	5 mL
1 Tb	½ oz	*	1½ cL	15 mL
¼ c	2 oz	½ dL	6 cL	59 mL
⅓ c	2⅔ oz	¾ dL	8 cL	79 mL
½ c	4 oz	1 dL	12 cL	119 mL
⅔ c	5⅓ oz	1½ dL	15 cL	157 mL
¾ c	6 oz	1¾ dL	18 cL	178 mL
1 c	8 oz	¼ L	24 cL	237 mL
1¼ c	10 oz	3 dL	30 cL	296 mL
1⅓ c	10⅔ oz	3¼ dL	33 cL	325 mL
1½ c	12 oz	3½ dL	35 cL	355 mL
1⅔ c	13⅓ oz	3¾ dL	39 cL	385 mL
1¾ c	14 oz	4 dL	41 cL	414 mL
2 c; 1 pt	16 oz	½ L	47 cL	473 mL
2½ c	20 oz	6 dL	60 cL	592 mL
3 c	24 oz	¾ L	70 cL	710 mL
3½ c	28 oz	⅘ L	83 cL	829 mL
4 c	32 oz	1 L	95 cL	946 mL
5 c	40 oz	1¼ L	113 cL	1134 mL
6 c	48 oz	1½ L	142 cL	1420 mL
8 c	64 oz	2 L	190 cL	1893 mL
10 c	80 oz	2½ L	235 cL	2366 mL
12 c	96 oz	2¾ L	284 cL	2839 mL
4 qt	128 oz	3¾ L	375 cL	3785 mL
5 qt	160 oz			
6 qt	192 oz			
8 qt	256 oz			

Length

⅛ in = 3 mm

¼ in = 6 mm

⅓ in = 1 cm

½ in = 1.5 cm

¾ in = 2 cm

1 in = 2.5 cm

1½ in = 4 cm

2 in = 5 cm

2½ in = 6 cm

4 in = 10 cm

8 in = 20 cm

10 in = 25 cm

Other Conversions

Ounces to milliliters: multiply ounces by 29.57

Quarts to liters: multiply quarts by 0.95

Milliliters to ounces: multiply milliliters by 0.034

Liters to quarts: multiply liters by 1.057

Ounces to grams: multiply ounces by 28.3

Grams to ounces: multiply grams by .0353

Pounds to grams: multiply pounds by 453.59

Pounds to kilograms: multiply pounds by 0.45

Cups to liters: multiply cups by 0.24

Temperatures

275°F = 140°C

300°F = 150°C

325°F = 170°C

350°F = 180°C

375°F = 190°C

400°F = 200°C

425°F = 215°C

450°F = 230°C

475°F = 240°C

500°F = 250°C

Index